Frantic Assembly and Theatre Royal Plymouth in collaboration with Royal & Derngate Northampton

SHAKESPEARE'S

OTHELLO

Adapted by Scott Graham and Steven Hoggett
for Frantic Assembly

This version of *Othello* was first performed on 20th September 2008 at Theatre Royal Plymouth.

franticassembly THEATRE ROYAL PLYMOUTH THEATRES ROYAL & DERNGATE NORTHAMPTON

CAST

Othello	**Jimmy Akingbola**
Iago	**Charles Aitken**
Desdemona	**Claire-Louise Cordwell**
Emilia	**Leila Crerar**
Cassio	**Jami Reid-Quarrell**
Roderigo	**Richard James-Neale**
Brabantio & Lodovico	**Marshall Griffin**
Montano	**Eddie Kay**
Bianca	**Minnie Crowe**

CREATIVE TEAM

Direction & Adaptation	**Scott Graham & Steven Hoggett**
Design	**Laura Hopkins**
Lighting Design	**Natasha Chivers**
Sound Design	**Gareth Fry**
Soundtrack	**Hybrid**
Choreography	**Scott Graham, Steven Hoggett & company**
Casting Director	**Sarah Hughes**
Dialect Coach	**Sally Hague**
Assistant Director	**Jamie Rocha Allan**
Associate Lighting Designer	**Andy Purves**
Assistant Designers	**Simon Kenny and Bronia Housman**

PRODUCTION TEAM

Production Manager	**Nick Ferguson**
Company Stage Manager	**Joni Carter**
Deputy Stage Manager	**Kerry Lynch**
Technical Stage Manager	**Nick Hill**

FOR THEATRE ROYAL PLYMOUTH

Production Manager	**David Miller**
Costume Supervisor	**Lorna Price**
Sets, Props & Costumes	**TR2 – Theatre Royal Plymouth Production Centre**

FOR FRANTIC ASSEMBLY

Producer	**Lisa Maguire**
Creative Learning & Admin Manager	**Laura Sutton**
Administrator	**Fiona Gregory**
Intern	**Katherine Tittley**
Creative Learning Associates	**Simon Pittman & Vicki Manderson**
Marketing	**Georgette Purdey, Sam McAuley & Mark Slaughter for makes three**
Press	**Clióna Roberts for crpr**
Production Image	**Perou**
Graphic Design	**John Pasche**
Rehearsal Photos	**Manuel Harlan**

Developed at the Lyric Hammersmith.

Frantic Assembly would like to thank the following people and places for their support with the creation of *Othello*:

Bryony Lavery, David Farr, Edyta Budnik, Francis Angol, Imogen Heap, Liz Heywood, Paul Crewes, Paulette Randall, Perou, Simon Stephens (Brit School), Simon Stokes, The Cock Tavern, The Jerwood Space, The Union Jack, The Tricycle Theatre, Tom Morris, 3one7, Eddie Kay, Georgina Lamb, Ifan Meredith, Mark Springer, Matti Houghton, Michael Camp and Mulika Ojikutu.

BIOGRAPHIES

SCOTT GRAHAM (Artistic Director) Scott Graham is co-founder and Artistic Director of Frantic Assembly. Director credits for the company include *Stockholm, pool (no water), Dirty Wonderland, Rabbit, Peepshow* and *Underworld.* Performer / Director credits include *Hymns, Tiny Dynamite, On Blindness, Heavenly, Sell Out, Zero, Flesh, Klub* and *Look Back In Anger.* Scott Graham's other directing credits include: *Home* (National Theatre of Scotland) and *It's A Long Road* and *Up on the Roof* (PolkaTheatre). Choreography and movement director credits include: *Frankenstein (*Royal & Derngate, Northampton); *The May Queen* (Liverpool Everyman); *Hothouse* and *Market Boy* (National Theatre); *Villette (*Stephen Joseph Theatre); *Vs* (Karim Tonsi Dance Company, Cairo); *Improper* (Bare Bones Dance Company); *Dazzling Medusa* and *A Bear Called Paddington* (Polka) and *Stuart Little* (No 1 tour). With Steven Hoggett and Bryony Lavery, Scott created *It Snows,* a National Theatre Connections play for 2008.

STEVEN HOGGETT (Artistic Director) Steven Hoggett is co-founder and Artistic Director of Frantic Assembly. Director credits for the company include *Stockholm, pool (no water), Dirty Wonderland, Rabbit, Peepshow* and *Underworld.* Performer / Director credits include *Hymns, Tiny Dynamite, On Blindness, Heavenly, Sell Out, Zero, Flesh, Klub* and *Look Back In Anger.* As Associate Director / Movement, Steven worked on the multi award-winning production *Black Watch* (National Theatre of Scotland). Other choreography and movement director credits include *365* (National Theatre of Scotland); *Frankenstein* (Royal & Derngate, Northampton); *Hothouse* and *Market Boy* (National Theatre); *The Bacchae* (National Theatre of Scotland); *Wolves in the Walls* (National Theatre of Scotland and Improbable); *Villette* (Stephen Joseph Theatre); *Jerusalem* (West Yorkshire Playhouse); *Mercury Fur* and *The Straits* (Paines Plough);*Vs* (Karim Tonsi Dance Company); *Waving* (Oily Carte) and *Improper* (Bare Bones Dance Company). Commercial work includes the award-winning *Relationships Dance* TV commercial for Orange. Additional performance credits include *Manifesto* (Volcano Theatre Company) and *Go Las Vegas* (The Featherstonehaughs). With Scott Graham and Bryony Lavery, Steven created *It Snows*, a National Theatre Connections play for 2008.

LAURA HOPKINS (Designer) Frantic Assembly productions include: *Stockholm.* Theatre credits include: costume design for *Rudolf* (Raimond Theatre, Vienna); *Black Watch* (National Theatre of Scotland); *The Merchant of Venice* (Royal Shakespeare Company); *Peer Gynt* (Tyrone Guthrie Theatre, Minneapolis); *Kellerman* (Imitating the Dog and Pete Brooks); *Rough Crossings* and *Faust* (Headlong); *The Three Musketeers*, *Cinderella the Musical* and *Hamlet* (Bristol Old Vic); *Under the Black Flag, The Storm*, *Dido Queen of Carthage*, *The Golden Ass* and *Macbeth* (Shakespeare's Globe Theatre); *The Escapologist* (Suspect Culture, Tramway Glasgow); *Jerusalem* (2006 TMA Design Award, West Yorkshire Playhouse); *The Class Club* and *Office Party Xmas 2007* (Barbican); *Othello, Hamlet* and *Faustus* (2004 TMA Best Design Award, Royal & Derngate, Northampton); *Le Comte Ory* (Garsington); *Cosi fan Tutte* (English National Opera); *Carnesky's Ghostrain* (Truman Brewery, Brick Lane and Tour); *L'Elisir d'Amore* (New Zealand Festival/Opera), costumes for *Barber of Seville*

(Komische Oper Berlin) and *Mister Heracles* (TMA Best Design Award, West Yorkshire Playhouse).

NATASHA CHIVERS (Lighting Designer)
Frantic Assembly productions include: *pool (no water)*; *Dirty Wonderland*; *Tiny Dynamite*; *Peepshow*; *Hymns* and *Sell-Out*. Theatre credits include: *That Face* (The Duke of York's and Royal Court); *Statement Of Regret* (The National Theatre); *Electric Counterpoint* (Christopher Wheeldon/Royal Opera House); *Love* (Vesturport/ Lyric Hammersmith); *The Ballet Boyz – Encore and Greatest Hits* (Sadler's Wells/Tours); *Ballet for the People*, new pieces by Craig Revel-Horwood, Rafael Bonachela and Will Tuckett (The Royal Festival Hall); *The Wolves in the Walls* (National Theatre Of Scotland/Improbable/ Tramway/Tour/New York); *Home Glasgow* and *Mary Stuart* (National Theatre Of Scotland); *Playhouse Creatures* and *Jerusalem* (West Yorkshire Playhouse); *The Glass Cage* and *Twelfth Night* (Royal & Derngate, Northampton); *The Straits, Crazy Gary's Mobile Disco, The Drowned World, Mercury Fur, The Small Things* and *Pyrenees* (Paines Plough). Awards include: 2007 Olivier Award for Lighting Design, *Sunday In The Park With George* (The Wyndhams Theatre); *Beyond Belief* (Carriageworks, Sydney) Arts Council International Fellowship Award.

GARETH FRY (Sound Designer)
Gareth trained at the Central School of Speech & Drama in theatre design. Recent work includes: *Black Watch* (National Theatre of Scotland); *Some Trace of Her* and *Waves* (National Theatre); *Shun-kin* (Complicite); *The City* (Royal Court); *OK Computer* and *Jump* for Lu Kemp/BBC Radio 4. Other work includes: *Astronaut* (Theatre O); *Tangle, The Swing Left, Zero Degrees* and *Drifting* (Unlimited Theatre); *Almost Blue* (Riverside Studios, OSBTT); *The Watery Part of the World* (BAC); *Shadowmouth* and *Romans in Britain* (Sheffield Crucible); *The Bull, The Flowerbed* and *Giselle* (Fabulous Beast Dance Theatre, Barbican Theatre); *Living Costs* (DV8 at Tate Modern); *How Much is Your Iron?* and *The Jewish Wife* (Young Vic Brecht Fest); *O Go My Man, Talking to Terrorists* and *Macbeth* (Out of Joint); *The Overwhelming* (Laura Pels Theatre, NY). For the Royal Court: *Harvest, Forty Winks, Under the Whaleback, Night Songs, Face to the Wall, Redundant, Mountain Language, Ashes to Ashes, The Country*. For the National Theatre, England: *Fram, Women of Troy, A Matter Of Life and Death, Attempts on Her Life, Waves, The Overwhelming, Theatre of Blood, Fix Up, Iphigenia at Aulis, The Three Sisters, Ivanov* and *The Oresteia*. For Complicite: *Noise of Time* (with the Emerson String Quartet), *Strange Poetry* (with the LA Philharmonic Orchestra) and *Mnemonic* (associate). Events include: Somerset House Film4 Summer Screen & Ice Rink. Awards include: Laurence Olivier Award Sound Design 2007 for *Waves*. More info at www.garethfry.co.uk.

HYBRID (Soundtrack)
Mike Truman and Chris Healings have been writing, producing, touring and DJ-ing all over the globe for the best part of a decade and have amassed nearly 250 productions to date. The duo have written three LPs, *Wide Angle* which was released in 1999, *Morning Sci fi* released in 2003 and *I Choose Noise* in 2007 on Distinctive Records. They were chosen by Moby to support him on his Autumn 2000 North American tour which covered 43 dates over

56 days. This gave the fledgling band time to get ready for their first punishing global tour over 18 months, taking them to every venue that matters from as far afield as Australia, Japan for the Fuji Rock Festival, Melbourne for the Millennium NYE, across Europe and back to the UK to headline many festival tents and concert venues. Their second album's more fragile and darker sound has led to them getting involved with scoring for film and the duo worked with Harry Gregson Williams in January 2004 on Tony Scott's *Man on Fire*. Since then they have been involved in the production of the score for Ridley Scott's *Kingdom of Heaven* and the Tony Scott films, *Domino* and *Déjà Vu* and have recently completed their first solo score for Twisted Pictures newest production, *Catacombs*. Now touring as a full seven piece band, Hybrid spent last summer playing live in the US, Australia and Europe, working with Perry Farrell from Jane's Addiction, Peter Distefano from Porno For Pyros and Hooky from New Order. Now fronted by permanent singers Charlotte James and John Graham they are currently working on album four while busy with touring, film projects and a DJ compilation to be released this summer.

SARAH HUGHES (Casting Director)
Sarah has been Alan Ayckbourn's casting director for the last 17 years, casting all shows at the Stephen Joseph Theatre, and doing all Alan's other casting in the West End, on Broadway and elsewhere. She has worked part-time for the entertainment department at the BBC for the last seven years, where shows include *Fifteen Storeys High*, *Jonathan Creek*, *Love Soup* and *Pulling*. In addition, she freelances for a number of regional theatres and production companies, and also works as a lecturer.

JAMIE ROCHA ALLAN (Assistant Director)
Jamie trained on the MFA theatre director's course at Birkbeck. As part of this he spent a three month placement at Arts Educational Theatre School, he was Associate Director on *As You Like It*, directed by James Tillit, and also assisted Raz Shaw on the UK Premier of *Radium Girls*. While on secondment at the Lyric Hammersmith as the Resident Assistant Director, Jamie assisted David Farr on *Water, Metamorphosis* and *Arturo Ui* and assisted Paul Hunter on the Lyric's Christmas Show, *Beauty and the Beast*. He also directed two scratch performances, *In The Penal Colony* by Steven Berkoff – using four of the actors of the *Arturo Ui* cast – and a revised version of David Farr's *Crime and Punishment in Dalston*.

CHARLES AITKEN (Iago)
Charles trained at RADA. Theatre credits include: *Taming of the Shrew* (Wilton's Music Hall); *Midnight Cowboy* (Assembly Rooms, Edinburgh); *Paradise Lost* (Headlong); *Hair* (The Gate) – nominated for Best Newcomer by Whatsonstage.com and Theatre Goer Magazine – and *London Assurance* (Manchester Royal Exchange). Television credits include: *Bonkers* (ITV).

JIMMY AKINGBOLA (Othello)
Theatre credits include: *Look Back in Anger* (Jermyn Street Theatre); *White Open Spaces* (Pentabus/ Soho Theatre); *Henry VIII* (Royal Shakespeare Company/AandBC); *The Cut* (Donmar Warehouse); *After the End* (Paines Plough); *The Estate* (Cheltenham Literary Festival); *The Christ of Coldharbour Lane*, *3 Days in July,* and *Playing Fields* (Soho Theatre); *Prayer Room* (Birmingham Rep/Edinburgh Lyceum); *Blue/Orange* (Winner 2005 TMA Best Supporting Actor

Award – Sheffield Crucible); *People Next Door* (Edinburgh Traverse/Stratford East); *Thumbelina* (Stephen Joseph Theatre); *Naked Justice* (West Yorkshire Playhouse/ Tour); *Baby Doll* (National Theatre/ Albery Theatre); *The Changeling* (National Theatre); *Nativity, The Shooky* and *Behzti* (Birmingham Rep); *Ramayana* (National Theatre/ Birmingham Rep) and *Ready or Not* (Stratford East). Television and Film credits include: *Holby Blue; Holby City; Doctors, Who Killed PC Blakelock?; The Crouches, Roger Roger; Longford; Blackbeard; Stupid; The Bill; The Royal* and *The Slightly Filthy Show*. Radio credits include: *The Car; Anansi; The Dimples Cry; The Listener; Paid Servant; All American Boys; Eat Your Heart Out; Just Like Ronaldinho; Objects of Insane Desire; Ibadan; Troilus and Cressida; The Fire Children; A Noise in the Night; Clothes of Nakedness; Westway; Trinidad Sisters* and *Dancing Backwards.*

CLAIRE-LOUISE CORDWELL (Desdemona)
Claire-Louise trained at RADA. Theatre credits include: *Torn* (Arcola Theatre); *Dirty Butterfly* (Young Vic); *Days of Significance* (Royal Shakespeare Company); *Burn; Citizenship* (National Theatre); *Stoning Mary* (Royal Court Theatre) and *Compact Failure* (Clean Break Theatre Company). Television credits include: *EastEnders, Doctors, Casualty* (BBC); *Stuart: A Life Backwards* (Neal St Productions); *The Bill* (Talkback Thames); *Trial & Retribution* (La Plante Productions); *Bad Girls* (Shed Productions); *Jane Hall* (Granada) and *The Curry Club* (Sugar House Productions).

LEILA CRERAR (Emilia)
Leila trained at the Welsh College of Music and Drama. Theatre credits include: *Closer* and *Be My Baby* (The Dukes Playhouse, Lancaster); *The Visit* (winning the Lloyds Bank Theatre Challenge); *Frida and Diego* (National Theatre for MPYT); *Mental* (Edinburgh Festival); *The Method, Stone* and *Kay in Walls* (BAC); *Hippolytus* (Actors of Dionysus); *Jane Austen's Emma* (The Haymarket, Basingstoke); Steven Berkoff's *Sit and Shiver* (New End/ Hackney Empire) and *Les Liaisons Dangereuses* (The New Vic Theatre) and *Troilus and Cressida* and *Measure for Measure* (Theatr Clwyd). Film and television credits include: *Raging Angels* (MPYT); *Two Way Journey* (Solo Spot Productions) *Tales from Coney Island* (Blast Films); *Belonging* (BBC Wales) and *Doctors* (BBC).

MINNIE CROWE (Bianca)
Minne trained at the University of Birmingham and Central School of Speech and Drama. Theatre credits include: *Return to the Forbidden Planet* (Queen's Theatre, Hornchurch); *Match Fixing* (Union Theatre); *When the Lights Went Out* (Tara Arts/Tour); *We're Going on a Bear Hunt* (Polka Theatre/ Lakeside Arts Centre); *Eddie and Sissy* (Queen's Theatre Hornchurch); *Habeas Corpus* (The Peter Hall Company/ Theatre Royal Bath/ No 1 Tour); *Ali Baba and the Forty Thieves* (London Bubble TC); *Wait Until Dark* (Bill Kenwright Ltd/ No 1 Tour); *The People Are Friendly* (Queen's Theatre Hornchurch); Ella in *Cinderella* (London Bubble TC/ Greenwich Theatre Royal); Ruskin in *Krindlekrax* (Queen's Theatre Hornchurch); *Alice Through the Looking Glass* (London Bubble TC/ Open Air Tour) and *Coriolanus* (Crescent Theatre Birmingham). Film credits include: *Blood Red Letters* (NT Films).

MARSHALL GRIFFIN (Brabantio & Lodovico)
Marshall recently appeared as Junius Brutus in *Coriolanus*

and Biff Loman in *Death of a Salesman* at the Mercury Theatre Colchester. Previous theatre includes *The Adventures of Robin Hood* (Tobacco Factory Bristol); *Twelfth Night* and *Four Nights in Knaresborough* (Octagon Theatre Bolton) for which he was nominated Best Actor in a Leading Role at the Manchester Evening News Theatre Awards. He has also appeared in the title role of *Henry V* (Union Theatre); *Baby Doll* (National Theatre) and *Antigone* (Donmar Warehouse/Old Vic). Film credits include *Zone 3* (Two Suns Productions); *Camp X-Ray* (GV Motion Pictures); *Gas* (Polaris Productions); *Standing Corner* (Angelic Films) and *Dance of Shiva* (Epiphany Productions). TV credits include *Island at War* (Granada TV); *Submerged* (NBC); *Bad Blood* (Urban/Autumn Productions) and of course... *The Bill*. Radio credits include *The History Man* for Radio 4.

RICHARD JAMES-NEALE (Roderigo)
Richard trained at Mountview Academy of Theatre Arts, graduating with a first class honours degree in June 2006. Whilst at Mountview, he was nominated for the 2006 Spotlight Prize and was a commended finalist in the 2006 BBC Carlton Hobbs Radio Competition. Theatre credits include: *Pygmalion* (Old Vic); *Cyrano de Bergerac* (Royal Shakespeare Company); *A Midsummer Night's Dream* and *The Tempest* (UK and International Tours); *A Midsummer Night's Dream* and *The Comedy of Errors* (Ludlow Castle); *Thickness of Skin* (Chelsea Theatre); *Brenda Bly Teen Detective* (Pleasance Theatre, Islington); *The Threepenny Opera* (Lyric Hammersmith) and *Murder in the Cathedral* (Southwark Cathedral and Westminster Cathedral both with the National Youth Theatre) and *The 24 Hour Plays: Red Bull Sessions* (Tabard Theatre). Film and television credits include: *The Insiders* (Twenty Twenty Productions/Channel 4) and work as a voiceover artist (BBC Active). www.richardjames-neale.co.uk.

EDDIE KAY (Montano)
Eddie Kay trained at London Contemporary Dance School and Northern School of Contemporary Dance. Frantic Assembly productions include: *Hymns* and *Dirty Wonderland*. Theatre Credits include: *Tracker* (Broken Talkers); *Shadowmouth* (Sheffield Crucible); *Tranny-Boy* (Legs on the Wall); *Cost of Living* (DV8 Physical Theatre); *Awkward Project* (Bobs Your Uncle) and Attic Dance Company (1996 – 2000). TV credits include: Eurovison Song Contest (Dustin the Turkey – Ireland); *Round 10* (4 Dance); and *Cost of Living* (DV8 Films). Eddie choreographed *Round 10* (4 Dance) and directed *Crash Test Human* (Freshmess); *Paper Dogs* and *Dirty Priests* (big man wee man). He is co-director of big man wee man.

JAMI REID-QUARRELL (Cassio)
Jami trained in acting at the Actors Lab in Glasgow, with Tom Grail in New York, and in physical theatre with Blue Raincoat Theatre Ireland, The Circus Space and Centre des Artes du Cirque in France. Theatre Credits include the title role in *MONKEY!* (West Yorkshire Playhouse); *Midsummer Nights Dream* (Royal Opera House); *Equus* (David Pugh Productions); *The Firebird Ball* (Punchdrunk); *The Tempest*, *The Winter's Tale* and *Pericles* (Royal Shakespeare Company); *The Little Mermaid* (Sphinx Theatre); *Legend of Tarzan* (Metropolis Productions, Dubai); *L'Etourdie* (Les Fetes Nocturnes, Chateau de Grignan); *Scrooge* (Blue Raincoat Theatre Company); *The Girl from the Sea* (EPC); *Oedipus at Colonus* and *Who's Afraid of*

Virginia Woolf? (Actors Lab). Physical Theatre credits include *Under the Radar* (Jess Curtis Gravity); *Touch don't Touch* (Blue Eyed Soul); *Arena* and *Sounding Off* (Emergency Exit Arts); *Fledgling* (CB Projects); *Figure, Fit to Fill* (FAQ) and *Invitro* (Archaos). Opera credits as an actor/dancer include *Betrothal at a Monastery* (Glyndebourne) and *Alceste* (Scottish Opera). Television includes *Boy Kill Boy* (No Conversation); *Bunnytown* (Baker Coogan Productions); *Taggart* and *High Road* (STV); *Mark Thomas Comedy Product* and *Who do you think you are* (The Spice Girls). Commercials for Solpadeine, Smith's Menswear, Always, Beamish Red and Black. Film includes *28 Weeks Later*; *Khabi Alveida Naa Khena*; *Jhoom Barabar Jhoom*; *Under the Rainbow*; *Bent*; *Silent Scream*; *Arch Enemy*; *TodayTomorrowForever*.

ANDY PURVES (Associate Lighting Designer)
Andy trained in lighting design and theatre making at Central School of Speech and Drama where he also tutors in lighting. Frantic Assembly productions include: lighting design for *Stockholm* and production electrics and relights for *pool (no water)*. Andy is a lighting designer and creative technician working primarily in visual and movement based theatre and on projects in found space. Recent projects include lighting for *Office Party* (Underbelly, Edinburgh and Barbican Pit Theatre); lighting design for *Frankenstein* (Royal & Derngate, Northampton); production electrics on *The Maids* (Brighton Festival); technical management and lighting for *Bless* and *Cooped* (Spymonkey); lighting and technical design for *Outré*, dance and live music event by Array with Warp Records artists (Brighton Festival and Edinburgh Fringe 2006); production electrics and relighting for *The Wolves in the Walls* (National Theatre of Scotland and Improbable); lighting design for *Home Inverness* (National Theatre of Scotland); lighting and scenography for *A Devilish Exercise* (Rose Theatre site); lighting for *Almost Blue* (Oxford Samuel Beckett Theatre Trust Award Winner, Riverside Studios); spatial and lighting design for *Dreams Come Out to Play* (Knavish Speech, Edinburgh Fringe 2005 and Birmingham Rep); lighting, technical design and scenography for found space dance event Ren-Sa (Array, Edinburgh Fringe 2005). Andy was presented with awards for lighting design and technical excellence at the National Student Drama Festival 2005.

NICK FERGUSON (Production Manager)
Nick has been working in theatre for 30 years. His career has spanned commercial, classical and fringe theatre, film and television. Frantic Assembly productions include *Stockholm*. Nick has worked with Edinburgh's homeless and disaffected with the Grass Market Project, as well as with directors like Peter Stein, Rufus Norris, Dame Judi Dench, Sir Derek Jacobi, Sir Antony Sher, Sacha Wares, Nancy Meckler and Adrian Noble. Nick spent four years working with Kenneth Branagh's Renaissance Theatre Company as Technical Director, he regularly production manages for the National Youth Theatre and also spent two years as a Project Manager at the Millennium Dome on the Our Town Story project along side the Richard Rogers Partnership. He is now a freelance Production Manager working with the Royal Shakespeare Company and Thelma Holt amongst others. Nick has worked in the US and Canada, Russia and Europe and in the Far East.

JONI CARTER (Company Stage Manager)
Frantic Assembly productions include: *Hymns; pool (no water)* and *Stockholm*. Joni works as a freelance stage manager / company manager on theatre projects and live events. Most recently she worked at the Royal Opera House on *Monkey – Journey to the West*. Other theatre credits include: LIFT 2008, Shakespeare's Globe Theatre 2004 – 2005 season. The Young Vic on *Vernon God Little* and *generations*, ENO and English Touring Opera, Theatre O on *Three Dark Tales* and *The Argument*. Joni has collaborated with the National Theatre, Tall Stories, Unicorn Theatre, Talawa and Theatre-Rites on projects and workshops created for young people. Joni has also project managed live events and installations at the Tate Modern and Royal Festival Hall.

NICK HILL (Technical Stage Manager)
Nick trained at Mountview Academy of Theatre Arts. Frantic Assembly productions include *Stockholm.* He has had a variety of work and life experience prior to his involvement with theatre: photographic sales to bus driving or backpacking to yogic retreats. An interest in staging theatre developed whilst working for Brighton Festival and Brighton Dome Theatre. He works regularly for the National Youth Theatre and The Comedy School. Alongside this he also regularly works in a variety of roles in the west end, recent productions are *Amy's View*, *Treats* (Garrick) and *Les Miserables* (Queens). He has also worked with TAPS (Television & Training Showcase, Shepperton Studio) on their live audience showcases.

KERRY LYNCH (Deputy Stage Manager)
Kerry graduated from the University of Surrey, Roehampton with a BA (hons) in Drama, Theatre, and Performance Studies, before training in Stage Management and Technical Theatre at the London Academy of Music and Dramatic Arts (LAMDA). Since graduating she has a worked as a freelance stage manager on the following projects: *Enemies* (Almeida Theatre); *Diamond Hard* (WRITE project Almeida Theatre); *Guys and Dolls* (UK tour); *Shadowlands* (UK tour/Wyndhams Theatre); *The Sea* (Theatre Royal Haymarket) and *Dickens Unplugged* (Comedy Theatre).

We hope you enjoy the production and would love to get your feedback. You can post your own review in the Othello forum on the Frantic Assembly website and join the mailing list to keep up to date with future Frantic Assembly productions and workshops

http://www.franticassembly.co.uk/forum.

OTHELLO PARTNERS

THEATRE ROYAL PLYMOUTH AND ROYAL & DERNGATE NORTHAMPTON

Frantic Assembly has regularly performed at the Drum Theatre Plymouth since 2000 and have co-produced with them on a number of occasions: *Peepshow* (2002), *Rabbit* (2003), *pool (no water)* (2006) and most recently the acclaimed production of *Stockholm* (2007). It has proved an inspiring and productive partnership. To build on this success and to develop their work together further Frantic Assembly and Plymouth collaborate once again for *Othello*. With this ambitious production the company moves from the 150-200 seat Drum to the much larger Theatre Royal stage for the first time.

'Thrilling, vigorous, tough and funny…one of the best pieces of physical theatre I've seen'
The Sunday Times on *Peepshow*

Photograph: Perou

Photograph: Robert Day

Scott Graham and Steven Hoggett joined forces with Royal & Derngate's Artistic Director Laurie Sansom to provide movement direction for *Frankenstein* earlier this year. Frantic Assembly is delighted to return to the Royal stage with another fresh take on a classic text and look forward to working together to develop audiences in Northampton and throughout the East Midlands.

'Laurie Sansom's fluid production creates a visually exciting phantasmagoria to bring the two worlds together and exploit Frantic Assembly's physical-theatre skills'
The Sunday Times on *Frankenstein*

OTHELLO TOUR 2008:

Theatre Royal Plymouth	20 – 27 September
The Lowry	30 September – 4 October
Royal & Derngate	7 – 18 October
Nuffield Theatre	21 – 25 October
Lyric Hammersmith	4 – 22 November

franticassembly

'The indefatigably inventive Frantic Assembly'

Frantic Assembly produces thrilling, energetic and uncompromising theatre.

The company makes work that reflects contemporary culture and attracts new audiences. In collaboration with a wide variety of artists, Frantic Assembly's Artistic Directors – Scott Graham and Steven Hoggett – create new work that places equal emphasis on movement, design, music and text. Since its formation in 1994, Frantic Assembly has toured extensively throughout the UK and internationally, building its reputation as the country's leading movement theatre company. Frantic Assembly has collaborated with some of the UK's best contemporary writers including Abi Morgan, Michael Wynne, Mark Ravenhill and Bryony Lavery.

Frantic Assembly operates a UK-wide Creative Learning and Training Programme, introducing over 3,500 participants each year to the company's methods of creating theatre, developing their physical performance skills and promoting confidence through achievement. In 2008 Frantic Assembly launched *IGNITION* – a highly physical and unique creative vocational training initiative for young men aged 16 – 20.

Photograph: Matthew Andrews

Photograph: Manuel Harlan

'An unforgettable piece of theatre for those lucky enough to witness it' *The Daily Telegraph* on *Dirty Wonderland*

Scott Graham	Artistic Director
Steven Hoggett	Artistic Director
Lisa Maguire	Executive Producer
Laura Sutton	Creative Learning & Admin Manager
Georgina Lamb	Creative Associate
Neil Bettles	Creative Associate – Ignition

Creative Learning Practitioners: Delphine Gaborit, Eddie Kay, Helen Heaslip, Imogen Knight, Karl Sullivan, Leon Baugh, Michael Camp, Simon Pittman, Steve Kirkham, Vicki Manderson.

www.franticassembly.co.uk

Stockholm by Bryony Lavery (2007)
A Frantic Assembly and Drum Theatre Plymouth production and UK tour. Revived in 2008 for performances at Brighton Festival and Hampstead Theatre.

pool (no water) by Mark Ravenhill (2006)
A Frantic Assembly, Drum Theatre Plymouth and Lyric Hammersmith production and UK tour.

Dirty Wonderland scripted by Michael Wynne and devised by the Company (2005)
Commissioned by Brighton Festival, a sell-out, site-specific production at the Grand Ocean Hotel, Saltdean.

Hymns by Chris O'Connell (1999/2000, revived in 2005)
Original production commissioned by the Gantry, Southampton Arts Centre, and produced in association with Lyric Hammersmith; toured the UK, Columbia, Italy, Ireland and Taiwan.

On Blindness by Glyn Cannon (2004)
A Frantic Assembly, Paines Plough and Graeae production and UK tour.

Rabbit by Brendan Cowell (2003)
A Frantic Assembly and Drum Theatre Plymouth production supported by Lakeside Arts Centre; toured for three months in the UK.

Peepshow by Isabel Wright (2002)
A Frantic Assembly, Drum Theatre Plymouth and Lyric Hammersmith production supported by Barclays Stage Partners; toured the UK and sold out during its three-week London run.

Heavenly by Scott Graham, Steven Hoggett and Liam Steel (2002)
Toured the UK, and played Soho Theatre, after several international dates, played off-Broadway for three weeks.

Tiny Dynamite by Abi Morgan (2001)
A Frantic Assembly, Paines Plough and Contact production; winner of Best Fringe Production Manchester Evening News Awards and Best Theatre Show, *City Life* Magazine; toured UK, Edinburgh Fringe, London, Bulgaria, Lithuania and Italy.

Underworld by Nicola McCartney (2001)
Toured the UK, London and Slovakia.

Sell Out by Michael Wynne (1998)
A UK tour culminated in a West End run at the New Ambassadors Theatre, for which it won the Time Out Live Theatre Award; toured Finland, France, Zimbabwe, Lebanon, Syria and Ireland.

Generation Trilogy (1998)
Klub, Flesh and Zero; toured throughout the UK in summer 1998.

Zero devised by the company (1998)
First performed in Edinburgh and toured the UK, Holland, Switzerland, Austria, Singapore and Hungary.

Flesh by Spencer Hazel (1996/97)
Toured the UK and Europe; a hit in Edinburgh and in Germany Italy, Spain, Hungary and Holland.

Klub by Spencer Hazel (1995/96)
First performed in Edinburgh; toured the UK and played in Ecuador and Egypt.

Look Back in Anger by John Osborne adapted by Spencer Hazel (1994)
First performed in Edinburgh; toured the UK until September 1995.

THEATRE ROYAL

PLYMOUTH THEATRES

"It's a blessing for people who have a passion for theatre to be able to feel part of the Theatre Royal, to be round like-minded people, to express themselves artistically, to be challenged and learn and be pushed out of their comfort zones."
(*Participant, People's Company*)

The **THEATRE ROYAL PLYMOUTH** is the largest and best attended regional producing theatre in the UK and the leading promoter of theatre in the South West. There are two distinctive performance spaces, the Theatre Royal itself and the Drum Theatre, as well as TR2, our award-winning Production and Creative Learning Centre.

The breadth of work presented and produced on the **THEATRE ROYAL** stage is extensive and includes contemporary and classic drama as well as very large-scale musicals. We also present leading national opera, ballet and dance companies.

"Plymouth is regularly playing host to some of the most exciting theatre in the UK."
(*The Guardian*)

The Theatre Royal plays a major role in producing and premiering high-quality theatre with an unusual range of partners. Recently, we have worked with Complicite to launch *A Disappearing Number* to international touring and wide acclaim. We have collaborated with Cameron Mackintosh to deliver the worldwide tour of Disney's *Mary Poppins* and have staged a first production of *Flashdance The Musical* for an initial UK tour. We have also worked with Matthew Bourne on the world premiere, in Plymouth, of his new production *Dorian Gray*, prior to performances at the Edinburgh International Festival and Sadlers Wells in London.

The **DRUM THEATRE** has become a creative driving force in the South West and beyond, pioneering new forms of stage writing, physical theatre and other innovative work. It has taken a leading role in an ongoing national exploration of new ways of producing and seeing theatre. In both 2002 and 2005 the Drum was nominated for the prestigious Peter Brook Empty Space Award for studio theatres. In 2007, the Drum Theatre won it.

"The Drum is part of a change and is in the forefront of it, acting with a generosity of spirit that puts art and artists centre stage"
(*The Guardian*)

At the forefront of the development of creative partnerships, the Drum has had an exciting and ongoing relationship with Frantic Assembly over a ten year period and has built a voracious appetite, amongst young and

THEATRE ROYAL
PLYMOUTH THEATRES

adult audiences, for Scott and Steven's unique brand of experiment and approach to theatre-making.

The Drum has collaborated with several other leading touring companies including Gecko, Paines Plough, ATC and Suspect Culture as well as co-producing with theatre partners such as the Tron in Glasgow, the Traverse in Edinburgh, the Royal Court, the Lyric Hammersmith and Hampstead Theatre. The Drum's programme has been augmented with weekly residencies from, amongst many others, Graeae, Told By An Idiot, Tim Crouch and Hoipolloi. The Theatre Royal's Young Company and People's Company have residency in the Drum Theatre and perform there at least three times a year.

"You only have to look around British theatre to see the Drum's fingerprints everywhere." *(The Guardian)*

Recent Drum Theatre productions include new plays by Doug Lucie, Simon Bent, Mark Ravenhill, Rona Munro, Chris Goode, Bryony Lavery, Robin Soans and Lucinda Coxon.

TR2, our production and education centre, is a unique facility. This architecturally award-winning waterfront building contains unrivalled set, costume, prop-making and rehearsal facilities. Some of the Theatre's most important and vigorous work is initiated by our Creative Learning team. Collaborating very extensively with communities in Plymouth and beyond, we provide projects and performances in the Theatres and elsewhere, often working with young people in formal education systems and beyond.

"An island in the dark stormy sea of the rest of my life."
(Participant, My Space, homelessness project)

Chief Executive	Adrian Vinken OBE
Artistic Director	Simon Stokes
Production and Technical Director	Jasper Gilbert
General Manager	Alvin Hargreaves
Development Director	Alice Cooper
Marketing & Sales Director	Marianne Smith
Creative Learning Director	Victoria Allen
Theatre Manager	Jack Mellor
Artistic Associate	David Prescott
Production Managers	Nick Soper & David Miller
Head of Workshop	Tony Harvey
Head of Wardrobe	Dina Hall
Technical Co-ordinator	Mark Hawker
PR Manager	Anne-Marie Clark (01752 230479)
Finance Manager	Paul James

"I can think of few arts complexes that induce such a rush of excitement on arrival." *The Daily Telegraph*

Royal & Derngate is the main venue for arts and entertainment in Northamptonshire.

In its two auditoria – the Royal auditorium seats 530 and the Derngate auditorium seats 1200-1400 people – the venue offers a diverse programme of work with everything from drama to dance, stand-up comedy to classical music, children's shows to opera on its stages. Some of the biggest names and productions on tour can be found here, alongside a programme of widely acclaimed in-house produced work.

This season, as well as collaborating on *Othello*, we also produced a vibrant reworking of Muriel Sparks' popular novel *The Prime of Miss Jean Brodie*, and at Christmas, we'll pack the venue with a kaleidoscope of colour as we visit the Emerald City in *The Wizard of Oz*.

We play host to innovative events such as the 30th Birthday Bash of Australian circus troupe Circus Oz and a unique live performance combining ambient electronica with orchestral music from The Bays and The Heritage Orchestra, as well as more familiar productions including the spectacular musical *Cabaret* and theatrical sensation, *Stomp*. The Royal Philharmonic Orchestra also continue their residency with us with another season of classical music featuring a Best Of British programme, The Third Annual Malcolm Arnold Festival and Verdi's irrepressible *Requiem*.

The theatre also offers a programme of Creative Projects that give audiences the chance to get involved in performing, writing or to find out more about what goes on behind the scenes.

Every year more than 350,000 people visit Royal & Derngate: we hope that we will welcome you through our doors this year.

To find out more about our programme of events call our Box Office on 01604 624811 or visit our website at www.royalandderngate.co.uk

PRAISE FOR SOME OF ROYAL & DERNGATE'S PRODUCTIONS:

Follies 2006

"...Laurie Sansom's superb production" ★★★★
The Guardian

Nominated for the TMA Best Musical Production Award and Whatsonstage Best Regional Production Award

The Glass Cage 2007

"...Laurie Sansom's first-rate production"
The Guardian

101 Dalmatians 2007

"...just the right sort of bounding energy..."
The Times

The Clean House 2008

"...every aspect of this show is first-rate. It's a long time since I've seen anything better."
Oxford Times

Humble Boy 2008

"...brilliantly executed and hugely enjoyable."
Birmingham Post

James and The Giant Peach 2008

"In terms of uplifting family entertainment, this is as good as it gets."
Birmingham Post

Frankenstein 2008

"Shelley's story is slickly reborn by Evans for the 21st century"
The Times on *Frankenstein*

REHEARSAL PHOTOGRAPH

Photograph: Manuel Harlan

Artistic Director's Notes

It seems a long time ago that Tom Morris suggested we should do *Othello*. He said it would be right up our street as we were obsessed with sex, jealousy and the destruction of friendships. Once the moral and artistic indignation subsided we had to admit that he had a point. We probably were obsessed with those issues.

Several years later whilst developing work with Mark Ravenhill he introduced us to the book *Dark Heart, The Shocking Truth About Hidden Britain* by Nick Davies. The book touched us with its tales of dissolution and disenfranchisement, disturbingly chronicling racial and social tension in the UK's underbelly. Initially we wondered how *Dark Heart* itself might transfer to the stage. A later conversation saw us develop the idea of bringing the two worlds of *Othello* and *Dark Heart* together. This unlikely coupling immediately began to resonate with us. It seemed that this hybrid allowed us to create a story in a pub that followed the narrative arc of *Othello* rather than simply setting *Othello* in a pub.

Since then Lisa Maguire has worked tirelessly to find ways of bringing this project to life. Her enthusiasm, determination and belief have been matched only by Simon Stokes and his fantastic team at Plymouth Theatre Royal. It is their championing of our cause and their trust in us that has made this possible. If we could be more than eternally grateful then we would be.

We are now well into rehearsals. When we are not making our cast kick lumps out of each other and throw each other around we are sitting at a table and finding ways of bringing this adaptation to life. The input of our cast, creatives and stage management team into every level of the production is invigorating. Each day, as directors and adaptors of the text, we are being challenged, supported, questioned, encouraged and inspired. For us this process is educational and vital. Most of all it is truly collaborative. Every day builds a stronger respect for the words of *Othello* and the performers who are helping to create this production.

We are using the music of Hybrid to soundtrack *Othello*. We have waited years to make a show that matched the Hybrid sound – a fantastic fusion of the cinematic, the orchestral and the dancefloor. This emotional and dramatic soundtrack is a key element in our creative process and it is a rare privilege to be resourced so richly. The sounds of the pub are also a vital component in creating this world and to this end we have employed Gareth Fry on this project so who knows what might result here. The sounds of the estate, the running battles, the shattered glass, the screams, the barking dogs are just the beginning of that vocabulary.

It's a challenging project but our aim is to present an exciting and visceral *Othello* that grabs you, our audience, and blasts you through a tense and thrilling 90 minutes. We have not come to trash the Bard. Nor do we think he should be sanctified. The production is made with a love for the text and of its theatrical possibilities. The trails of little lives have also been an obsession of ours and the transposing of the action from Venice/Cyprus to a pub on a predominantly white rundown estate in West Yorkshire just made sense to us.

Ultimately, we have been selfish in aiming to create the kind of *Othello* that truly excites us. However, our end point is anything but selfish. We truly hope our *Othello* connects with you.

REHEARSAL SKETCH BY SCOTT GRAHAM

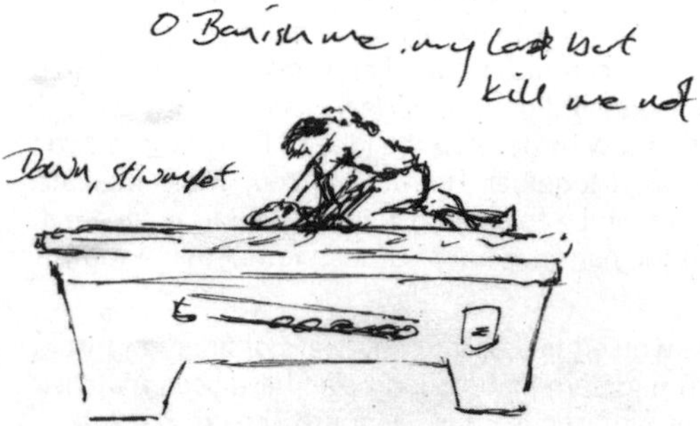
O Banish me, my lord but
kill me not
Down, strumpet

O+D in bed
while boys
continue
to play pool
around them

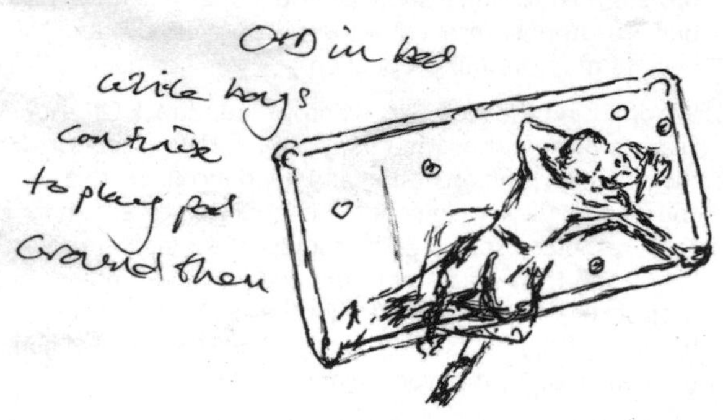

REHEARSAL PHOTOGRAPH

Photograph: Manuel Harlan

OTHELLO SOUND SKETCH BY STEVEN HOGGETT AND EDDIE KAY

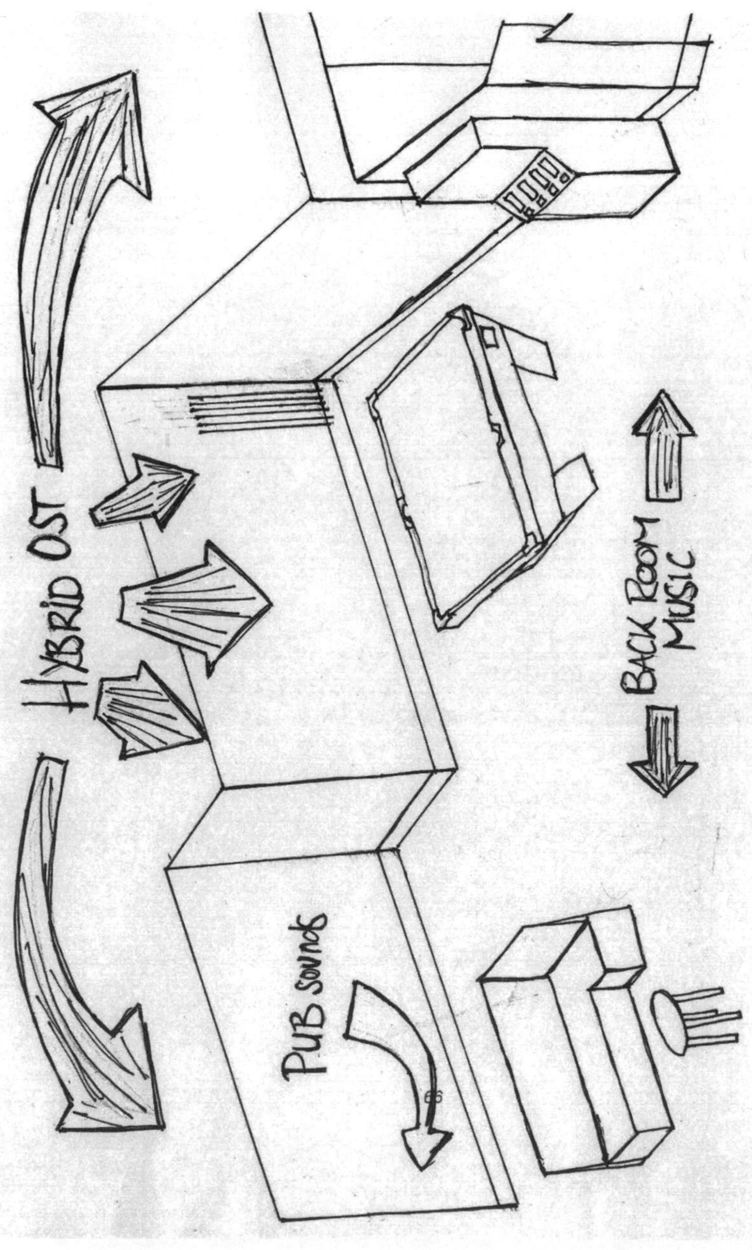

TRACK LISTING BY STEVEN HOGGETT

OTHELLO — Aug '08

Ph Overture ♪ Just For Today

Fruit Machine

Brabantio

Incoming

Ph Asian Invasion / Cassio's Lap ♪ Formula of Fear

Iago's ♀

3 Walls / Visionary

Ph Pool Table I. Sex / II Cue Balls ♪ All I Want??

Drunkard

Reputation / Cudgelled

~~~~

♪ I Choose Noise (strings) — Mini Overture

Reinstate → ♪ Keep It In The Family - edit

Men & Pool

Honky X△ x3

O - Blood³

Ph Mock Baroque ♪ Dogster

It's lost?

Dumb Show

Bianca Fondle

Ph Capsters ♪ Crime Boss ~~[illegible]~~

Cassio's Bauble

O Rage

Slapped

Vicious Triangle

Rodrigo Fight Plan

O - These ♀

Ph Prowler ♪ Prowler

Ph Toilet

Emilia & O ♪ Evacuating London

Stabs³

↓

? ♪ Just For Today - Strings Coda?

Empire of The Dead - Kicking?
~~~~

REHEARSAL SKETCH BY SCOTT GRAHAM

The Ottoman! (A brick comes through the window)

OTHELLO

First published in this adaptation in 2008 by Oberon Books Ltd
Reprinted in 2008
521 Caledonian Road, London N7 9RH
Tel: 020 7607 3637 / Fax: 020 7607 3629
e-mail: info@oberonbooks.com
www.oberonbooks.com

A catalogue record for this book is available from the British Library.

ISBN: 978-1-84002-856-0

Cover design by John Pasche

Cover photograph by Perou

Printed in Great Britain by CPI Antony Rowe, Chippenham.

Characters

OTHELLO

IAGO

DESDEMONA

EMILIA

CASSIO

RODERIGO

LODOVICO

MONTANO

BIANCA

BRABANTIO

West Yorkshire, 2001

Pre Show. A Thunderstorm.

Overture. (Includes these images.)

Introducing Pub Life.

BRABANTIO and his daughter DESDEMONA.

IAGO buys drinks for DESDEMONA with RODERIGO's money.

BRABANTIO and OTHELLO drink together.

OTHELLO evicts thugs. Has a fight. CASSIO backs him up. IAGO arrives too late. OTHELLO shows his appreciation.

OTHELLO and DESDEMONA - they are good together. We like them.

What IAGO sees – details, paranoia and opportunism.

DAY 1

RODERIGO and IAGO. IAGO is playing the fruit machine. He has a pint of lager on the top. Occasionally he taps RODERIGO for more coins.

At some point BRABANTIO is seen entering.

RODERIGO
Tush, never tell me! I take it much unkindly
That thou, Iago, who hast had my purse
As if the strings were thine, shouldst know of this.

IAGO
Sblood, but you will not hear me! If ever I did dream
Of such a matter, abhor me.

RODERIGO
It cannot be that Desdemona should love Othello. What should I do? I confess it is my shame to be so fond –

OTHELLO
(Passing.)
Good Iago!

IAGO
My noble lord… These moors are changeable in their wills –

IAGO stops as OTHELLO enters with DESDEMONA. DESDEMONA sees her father and drags OTHELLO into the women's toilets.

RODERIGO

Thou toldst me thou didst hold him in thy hate.

IAGO

Despise me, if I do not.
In personal suit to make me his lieutenant,
I off-capp'd to him: and, by the faith of man,
I know my price, I am worth no worse a place:
But he; as loving his own pride and purposes,
Evades me, with a bombast circumstance
Horribly stuff'd with epithets of war;
And, in conclusion,
Nonsuits me; for, 'Certes,' says he,
'I have already chose my officer.'
And what was he?
Forsooth, a great arithmetician,
One Michael Cassio,
A fellow
That never set a squadron in the field,
Nor the division of a battle knows
More than a spinster;
Mere prattle, without practice,
Is all his soldiership. But he, sir, had the election:
This counter-caster,
He, in good time, must his lieutenant be,
And I…?
Why, there's no remedy; 'tis the curse of service,
Preferment goes by letter and affection,
And not by old gradation, where each second
Stood heir to the first. Now, sir, be judge yourself,
Whether I in any just term am affined
To love the Moor.

RODERIGO

I would not follow him then.

IAGO

I follow him to serve my turn upon him:
In following him, I follow but myself;

I am not what I am.

RODERIGO
What a full fortune does the thicklips owe
If he can carry't thus!
Iago. What should I do? Desdemona?

He gestures towards BRABANTIO.

IAGO
Call up her father,
Rouse him: make after him, poison his delight,
Plague him with flies: though that his joy be joy,
Yet throw such changes of vexation on't,
As it may lose some colour.

RODERIGO
Brabantio! Brabantio!
Look to your house, your daughter and your bags!
Signior, is all your family within?

BRABANTIO
Why, wherefore ask you this?
Roderigo, I have charged thee not to haunt about my doors:
In honest plainness thou hast heard me say
My daughter is not for thee.

IAGO returns to the fruit machine. RODERIGO is looking for support. IAGO is not backing RODERIGO up.

RODERIGO
'Zounds, sir, you're robb'd; for shame,
Your heart has burst.
You have lost half your soul;
Even now, now, very now, an old black ram
Is tupping your white ewe.

BRABANTIO
What? Have you lost your wits?

IAGO
'Zounds, sir, you are one of those that will not serve God, if the devil bid you. Because we come to do you service and you

think we are ruffians, you'll have your daughter covered with a Barbary horse.

BRABANTIO

What profane wretch art thou?

IAGO

I am one, sir, that comes to tell you your daughter and the Moor are now making the beast with two backs.

BRABANTIO

This thou shalt answer.

IAGO

(*BRABANTIO grabs IAGO by the throat.*)

Straight satisfy yourself:
If she be in her chamber or our house.

BRABANTIO

(*To IAGO, threateningly.*)

Where is the Moor?

RODERIGO motions towards the women's toilets. BRABANTIO rushes in and emerges grappling with OTHELLO. OTHELLO restrains BRABANTIO.

O thou foul thief!

OTHELLO

Hold your hands.

MONTANO comes running in to see what the noise is. He, IAGO and RODERIGO make a show of their support for OTHELLO.

BRABANTIO

She is abused, stolen from me, ay, corrupted
By magic spells
To run from her guardage to the sooty bosom
Of such a thing as thou.
Judge me the world, if 'tis not gross in sense
That thou hast practised on her with foul charms,
Abused her delicate youth with drugs/

OTHELLO

That I have ta'en away this old man's daughter,
It is most true;

The very head and front of my offending
Hath this extent, no more.
Her father loved me, oft invited me
Still questioned me the story of my life
From year to year – the battles, sieges, fortunes
That I have passed.
I ran it through, even from my boyish days.
To th' very moment that he bade me tell it.
Send for the lady
And let her speak of me before her father:
If you do find me foul in her report,
The trust, the office I do hold of you,
Take away.

DESDEMONA comes out from the toilets.

BRABANTIO
I pray you, hear her speak
If she confess she was half the wooer,
Destruction on my head if my bad blame
Light on the man. Come hither, gentle mistress:
Do you perceive, in all this noble company
Where most you owe obedience?

DESDEMONA
I am your daughter: but here's my husband,
And so much duty as my mother show'd
To you, preferring you before her father,
So much I challenge that I may profess
Due to the Moor my lord.

BRABANTIO
God be wi' you! I have done.
I am glad at soul I have no other child:
Look to her, Moor, if thou hast eyes to see:
She has deceived her father, and may thee.

OTHELLO
My life upon her faith.

BRABANTIO exits. The boys mock him. OTHELLO shuts them up.

IAGO

(*Gesturing towards BRABANTIO.*)

Nine or ten times
I had thought t'have yerked him under the ribs. He prated
and spoke such scurvy and provoking terms
Against your honour…

OTHELLO

Let Him do his spite. My loyalty shall out-tongue his complaints.

MONTANO

(*Looking out of the window.*)

A Turkish fleet, bearing up to the Cypress!

IAGO

How many?

MONTANO

Fifty. A hundred?
Valiant Othello, we must employ you
Against the general enemy Ottoman.

OTHELLO

Cassio. Cassio!

CASSIO enters. He is dragging in LODIVICO who is bleeding. They have been taking on the Ottoman.

Suddenly a brick comes crashing through the window.

The pub springs to life. OTHELLO is pumped up ready for action. Everyone gets tooled up.

Honest Iago,
My Desdemona must I leave to thee

All the boys run out of the pub to fight.

IAGO is left with DESDEMONA and EMILIA and a nervous and shaken RODERIGO. The girls are thrilled with the situation and watch from a window.

RODERIGO

Iago, what will I do think'st thou?

IAGO

Why go to bed and sleep.

RODERIGO

I will drown myself.

IAGO

Drown thyself? O come, be a man.

RODERIGO

What should I do?

IAGO

Put money in thy purse. It cannot be that Desdemona should long continue to love the moor. She must change for youth: when she is sated with his body she will find the error of her choice. Therefore make money.
Go. Make money.

RODERIGO

Wilt thou be fast to my hopes, if I depend on the issue?

IAGO

Thou art sure of me. I have told thee often, and I tell thee again and again, I hate the Moor. My cause is hearted: thine hath no less reason.

RODERIGO

But…

IAGO

Let us be conjunctive in our revenge against him. If thou canst cuckold him, thou dost thyself a pleasure, me a sport. There are many events in the womb of time, which will be delivered.
Go. GO!
Put money enough in your purse.

RODERIGO runs off.

Thus do I ever make my fool my purse.
I hate the Moor
And it is thought about that 'twixt my sheets
He's done my office.
I know not if it be true.
But I for more suspicion in that kind will do as for surety.

He holds me well,
The better shall my purpose work on him.
Cassio's a proper man: let me see now
To get his place and to plume up my will
In double knavery. How? How?

The girls exit.

The walls peel back to reveal The Fight outside in the car park. IAGO remains playing pool, becoming more and more angry until he smashes the pool cue over the table. The Fight instantly ends and the walls return. IAGO is alone in the pool room.

There is banging at the fire exit. IAGO goes to it, opens it and CASSIO enters, does a lap of honour. The others, apart from OTHELLO, enter victorious.

CASSIO
(*Announcing his own entrance.*)
Michael Cassio,
Lieutenant to the warlike Moor Othello!

DESDEMONA
O behold,
The riches of the ship is come on shore!
What tidings can you tell me of my lord?

CASSIO
He's not arrived yet? He will be shortly here
Let it not gall your patience good Iago
That I extend my manners. 'Tis my breeding
That gives me this bold show of courtesy.

CASSIO kisses EMILIA.

IAGO
Sir, would she give you so much of her lips
As of her tongue she oft bestows on me,
You'll have enough.

DESDEMONA
Alas, she has no speech.

IAGO
In faith, too much;

I find it still, when I have list to sleep:
Marry, before your ladyship, I grant,
She puts her tongue a little in her heart,
And chides with thinking.

EMILIA
You have little cause to say so.

IAGO
Come on, come on; you are pictures out of doors,
Bells in your parlors, wild-cats in your kitchens,
Saints in your injuries, devils being offended,
Players in your housewifery, and housewives in your beds.

DESDEMONA
O, fie upon thee, slanderer!

IAGO
Nay, it is true, or else I am a Turk
You rise to play and go to bed to work.

EMILIA
You shall not write my praise.

IAGO
No, let me not.

DESDEMONA
What wouldst thou write of me, if thou shouldst praise me?

IAGO
O gentle lady, do not put me to't;
For I am nothing, if not critical.

DESDEMONA
Come, how wouldst thou praise me?

IAGO
I am about it; but indeed my invention
Comes from my pate as birdlime does from frize;
It plucks out brains and all: but my Muse labours,
And thus she is deliver'd.
If she be fair and wise, fairness and wit,
The one's for use, the other useth it.

DESDEMONA
Well praised! How if she be black and witty?

IAGO
If she be black, and thereto have a wit,
She'll find a white that shall her blackness fit.

DESDEMONA
Worse and worse.

EMILIA
How if fair and foolish?

IAGO
She never yet was foolish that was fair;
For even her folly help'd her to an heir.

DESDEMONA
These are old fond paradoxes to make fools laugh i' the alehouse. What miserable praise hast thou for her that's foul and foolish?

IAGO
There's none so foul and foolish thereunto,
But does foul pranks which fair and wise ones do.

DESDEMONA
O heavy ignorance! Thou praisest the worst best. But what praise couldst thou bestow on a deserving woman indeed, one that, in the authority of her merit, did justly put on the vouch of very malice itself?

IAGO
She that was ever fair and never proud,
Had tongue at will and yet was never loud,
Never lack'd gold and yet went never gay,
Fled from her wish and yet said 'Now I may,'
She that being anger'd, her revenge being nigh,
Bade her wrong stay and her displeasure fly,
She that in wisdom never was so frail
To change the cod's head for the salmon's tail;
She that could think and ne'er disclose her mind,
See suitors following and not look behind,
She was a wight, if ever such wight were –

DESDEMONA
To do what?

IAGO
To suckle fools and chronicle small beer.

DESDEMONA
O most lame and impotent conclusion! Do not learn of him, Emilia, though he be thy husband. How say you, Cassio, is he not a most profane and liberal counsellor?

CASSIO
He speaks home, madam, you may relish him more in the soldier than in the scholar.

IAGO
I have't, after some time to abuse Othello's ear
That he is too familiar with his wife.
The Moor is of a free and open nature
That thinks men honest that but seem to be so,
And will as tenderly be led by th'nose
As asses are.

A car horn goes in the car park.

MONTANO
The Moor!

CASSIO
'Tis truly so.

DESDEMONA
Let's meet him and receive him.

OTHELLO enters, DESDEMONA runs to him, jumps up and wraps her legs around him.

OTHELLO
The Turks are fucked!

Throwing his car keys to IAGO.

Go to the bay and disembark my coffers.

DESDEMONA
My dear Othello!

OTHELLO

O my souls joys. If after every tempest come such calms.
May the winds blow til they have wakened death,
And let the labouring bark climb hills of seas,
Olympus-high, and duck again as low
As hell's from heaven.
I prattle out of fashion, and I dote in mine own comforts.
Good Michael, look you to the guard tonight.

OTHELLO hands over authority to CASSIO by giving him his baseball bat.

IAGO

(*Taking the keys.*)
(*Aside.*) O you are well tuned now!
But I'll set down the pegs that make this music,
As honest as I am.

IAGO grabs RODERIGO and takes him into a corner.

First, I must tell thee this –Desdemona is directly in love with Cassio.

RODERIGO

With him! why, 'tis not possible.

IAGO

(*Putting his finger across RODERIGO's lips.*)
Lay thy finger thus, and let thy soul be instructed. Mark me with what violence she first loved the Moor, but for bragging and telling her fantastical lies: and will she love him still for prating? let not thy discreet heart think it. Her eye must be fed; and what delight shall she have to look on the devil? When the blood is made dull with the act of sport, there should be, again to inflame it, loveliness in favour, sympathy in years, manners and beauties; all which the Moor is defective in: now, for want of these required conveniences, her delicate tenderness will find itself abused, begin to heave the gorge, disrelish and abhor the Moor; very nature will instruct her in it and compel her to some second choice. Now, sir, this granted, who stands so eminent in the degree of this fortune as Cassio does? Why, none; why, none: the knave is handsome, young, and hath all those requisites in him that folly and green minds

look after: a pestilent complete knave; and the woman hath found him already.

RODERIGO

I cannot believe that in her; she's full of most bless't condition.

IAGO

Didst thou not see her paddle with the palm of his hand? Didst not mark that?

RODERIGO

Yes, that I did; but that was but courtesy.

IAGO

Lechery, by this hand; an index and obscure prologue to the history of lust and foul thoughts. They met so near with their lips that their breaths embraced together. Villanous thoughts, Roderigo! Sir, be you ruled by me. The lieutenant watches on the court of the guard. I'll not be far from you: do you find some occasion to anger Cassio. He is rash and very sudden in choler, and haply may strike at you: provoke him, that he may; for even out of that will I cause these of the Cypress to mutiny; whose qualification shall come into no true taste again but by the displanting of Cassio. And with the impediment most profitably removed, so shall you have a shorter journey to your desires.

RODERIGO

I will do this.

IAGO

I warrant thee. Fetch his necessaries ashore.

He gives OTHELLO's keys to RODERIGO. He watches as RODERIGO exits.

That Cassio loves her, I do well believe it;
That she loves him, 'tis apt and of great credit:
The Moor, howbeit that I endure him not,
Is of a constant, loving, noble nature,
And I dare think he'll prove to Desdemona
A most dear husband. Now, I do love her too;
Not out of absolute lust, though peradventure
I stand accountant for as great a sin,

But partly led to diet my revenge,
For that I do suspect the lusty Moor
Hath leap'd into my seat; the thought whereof
Doth, like a poisonous mineral, gnaw my inwards;
And nothing can or shall content my soul
Till I am even'd with him, wife for wife,
Or failing so, yet that I put the Moor
At least into a jealousy so strong
That judgment cannot cure.

He sees CASSIO.

I fear Cassio with my night-cap too –
Lieutenent! A stoup of wine?

CASSIO
Not tonight, good Iago.

IAGO
A measure to the health of black Othello.

CASSIO
I must to the watch.

IAGO
One cup…

IAGO entices him to drink.

OTHELLO is alone with DESDEMONA. It is a sexual/loving moment, completely unaware of the games about to start elsewhere.

OTHELLO
If I were now to die,
'Twere now to be most happy; for, I fear,
My soul hath her content so absolute
That not another comfort like to this
Succeeds in unknown fate.

DESDEMONA
The heavens forbid
But that our loves and comforts should increase
Even as our days do grow.

OTHELLO
Amen to that, sweet powers!

I cannot speak enough of this content,
It stops me here, it is too much of joy.
And this, and this the greatest discords be
That e'er our hearts shall make.

The boys are drinking.

IAGO
Another cup?

CASSIO
I have drunk two cups…and dare not task my weakness with any more.

IAGO
What, man! 'tis a night of revels…

CASSIO
I'l do it; but it dislikes me.

The atmosphere is getting more drunken and macho. CASSIO has obviously had a few and is getting a bit lairy. RODERIGO is watching, separate.

Well, God's above all; and there be souls must be saved, and there be souls must not be saved.

IAGO
It's true, good lieutenant.

CASSIO
For mine own part – no offence to the general, nor any man of quality – I hope to be saved.

IAGO
And so do I too, lieutenant.

CASSIO
Ay, but, by your leave, not before the lieutenant; Do not think, gentlemen. I am drunk:

RODERIGO laughs. CASSIO grabs him. Threatens him.

This is my right hand, and this is my left: I can stand well enough, and speak well enough. I am not drunk

RODERIGO
Excellent well.

CASSIO
Well then; you must not think then that I am drunk.

CASSIO goes back to play his shot. This is IAGO's moment. he gestures to RODERIGO. RODERIGO shakes his head. IAGO insists. RODERIGO is terrified but reaches out and knocks CASSIO's cue ruining his shot.

You rogue! You rascal!

CASSIO really lays into RODERIGO. It is brutal and shocking. There is broken glass everywhere. IAGO steps in.

IAGO
God's will, lieutenant, hold!
You will be shamed for ever.

MONTANO
Nay, good lieutenant. Hold your hand. (*Grabs CASSIO's arm.*)

CASSIO
Let me go sir, or I'll knock you o'er the mazzard.

MONTANO
Come, come, you're drunk.

CASSIO
Drunk!

CASSIO turns on MONTANO.

IAGO
Nay, good lieutenant. God's will, gentlemen!

CASSIO has lost the plot. OTHELLO rushes over.

OTHELLO
Hold for your lives!

MONTANO
I am hurt. He dies. (*Goes to attack CASSIO. OTHELLO stops him.*)

OTHELLO
Hold. He that stirs next to carve for his own rage

Holds his soul light. If I once stir, or do but lift this arm, the best of you shall sink in my rebuke.
Iago, who began this?

RODERIGO sneaks out.

IAGO
I do not know: friends all and then
Swords out, and tilting one at other's breast…

OTHELLO
How comes it Michael, you are thust forgot?

CASSIO
I pray you pardon me: I cannot speak. (*Throws up.*)

OTHELLO
Montano?…What's the matter,
That you unlace your reputation thus?

MONTANO
Iago can inform you.

OTHELLO
Iago on thy love I charge thee, who began this?

MONTANO
(*To IAGO.*) If thou dost deliver more or less than truth,
Thou art no soldier.

IAGO
I had rather have this tongue cut from my mouth
Than it should do offence to Michael Cassio;
Yet, I persuade myself, to speak the truth.
There comes Roderigo crying out for help:
And Cassio following him. Sir, this gentleman
Steps in to Cassio, and entreats his pause:
I found them close together,
At blow and thrust; even as again they were
When you yourself did part them.

OTHELLO
I know Iago, thy honesty and love
Doth mince this matter,
Making it light to Cassio

Cassio…never more be officer of mine.
Look if my gentle love be not raised up!
I'll make thee an example. (*Takes baseball bat off him. Sends him out. IAGO follows.*)

Outside. in the car park.

IAGO
What, are you hurt, lieutenant?

CASSIO
Ay, past all surgery.

IAGO
Marry, heaven forbid!

CASSIO
Reputation, reputation, reputation! O, I have lost my reputation! I have lost the immortal part of myself, and what remains is bestial. My reputation, Iago, my reputation!

IAGO
As I am an honest man, I thought you had received some bodily wound; there is more sense in that than in reputation. Reputation is an idle and most false imposition: oft got without merit, and lost without deserving: you have lost no reputation at all, unless you repute yourself such a loser. What, man! there are ways to recover the general again: sue to him and he's yours.

CASSIO
I will ask him for my place again; he shall tell me I am a drunkard! Had I as many mouths as Hydra, such an answer would stop them all. O God that men should put an enemy in their mouths to steal away their brains. That we with joy, pleasance, revel and applause transform ourselves into beasts. To be now a sensible man, by and by a fool and presently a beast. Every inordinate cup is unblessed and the ingredient is a devil. I, drunk!

IAGO
Come, come, you or any man living may be drunk at some time. Good wine is a good familiar creature, if it be well used: exclaim no more against it. I'll tell you what you shall do.

Our general's wife is now the general: confess yourself freely to her; importune her help to put you in your place again: she is of so free, so kind, so blessed a disposition, she holds it a vice in her goodness not to do more than she is requested: this broken joint between you and her husband entreat her to splinter.

CASSIO

You advise me well. Tomorrow I will beseech the virtuous Desdemona to undertake for me.

IAGO

You are in the right. Good night lieutenant.

CASSIO

Good night honest Iago.

CASSIO goes.

IAGO

And what's he then that says I play the villain
When this advice is free I give, and honest
Probal to thinking and indeed the course
To win the Moor again?
His soul is so enfettered to her love,
That she may make, unmake, do what she list
How am I then a villain
To counsel Cassio to this parallel course
Directly to his good?

IAGO is aware that someone is lurking in the shadows.

How now, Roderigo?

RODERIGO is in a bad way. CASSIO gave him a bit of a kick in.

RODERIGO

My money is almost spent; I have been tonight exceedingly well cudgelled; and I think the issue will be, I shall have so much experience for my pains, and so, with no money at all /

IAGO

How poor are they that have not patience!
Does't not go well? Cassio hath beaten thee.
And thou, by that small hurt, hast cashier'd Cassio:

Content thyself awhile…for whiles this honest fool
Plies Desdemona to repair his fortunes
And she for him pleads strongly to the Moor
I'll pour this pestilence into his ear
That she repeals him for her body's lust
And by how much she strives to do him good
She shall undo her credit with the Moor.

RODERIGO understands. He leaves.

So will I turn her virtue into pitch…
And out of her own goodness make the net
That shall enmesh them all.

DAY 2

Mini Overture.

DESDEMONA enters with EMILIA. They check that they are alone. DESDEMONA sits. There is a knock at the fire exit. EMILIA lets CASSIO in.

CASSIO
I am much bound to you.

EMILIA
Pray you come in,
I will bestow to you where you shall have time
To speak your bosom freely.

CASSIO
Bounteous madam,
Whatever shall become of Michael Cassio,
He's never any thing but your true servant.

DESDEMONA
I know't; I thank you. You do love my lord:
You have known him long; and be you well assured
He shall in strangeness stand no further off
Than in a polite distance.

CASSIO
Ay, but, lady,
That policy may either last so long,

Or feed upon such weak and waterish diet,
Or breed itself so out of circumstance,
That, I being absent and my place supplied,
My general will forget my love and service.

DESDEMONA
Do not doubt that; before Emilia here
I give thee warrant of thy place: assure thee,
If I do vow a friendship, I'll perform it
To the last article: my lord shall never rest;
I'll watch him tame and talk him out of patience;
His bed shall seem a school, his board a shrift;
I'll intermingle every thing he does
With Cassio's suit: therefore be merry, Cassio;
For thy solicitor shall rather die
Than give thy cause away.
Be thou assured, good Cassio, I will do
All my abilities in thy behalf.

EMILIA
Good madam, do, I warrant it grieves my husband
As if the cause were his.

DESDEMONA
Do not doubt, Cassio,
But I will have my lord and you again
As friendly as you were.

EMILIA
Madam, here comes my lord.

CASSIO
I'll take my leave.

DESDEMONA
Why, stay, and hear me speak.

Exit CASSIO.

Enter OTHELLO and IAGO. IAGO sets up the pool table.

IAGO
Ha! I like not that.

OTHELLO
What dost thou say?

IAGO
Nothing, my lord: or if – I know not what.

DESDEMONA
I have been talking with a suitor here,
A man that languishes in your displeasure.

OTHELLO
Who is't you mean?

DESDEMONA
Why, your lieutenant, Cassio. Good my lord,
If I have any grace or power to move you,
His present reconciliation take;
For if he be not one that truly loves you,
That errs in ignorance and not in cunning,
I have no judgment in an honest face:
I prithee, call him back.

OTHELLO
Not now, sweet Desdemona; some other time.

DESDEMONA
But shall't be shortly?

OTHELLO
The sooner, sweet, for you.

DESDEMONA
Shall't be tonight at supper?

OTHELLO
No, not tonight.

DESDEMONA
Why, then, to-morrow night; or Tuesday morn;
On Tuesday noon, or night; on Wednesday morn:
I prithee, name the time, but let it not
Exceed three days: in faith, he's penitent;
And yet his trespass, in our common reason –
Tell me, Othello: I wonder in my soul,
What you would ask me, that I should deny,

Or stand so mammering on. What! Michael Cassio,
That came a-wooing with you, and so many a time,
When I have spoke of you dispraisingly,
Hath ta'en your part; to have so much to do
To bring him in! Trust me, I could do much!

OTHELLO
Prithee, no more: let him come when he will;
I will deny thee nothing:
Whereon, I do beseech thee, grant me this,
To leave me but a little to myself.

DESDEMONA
Shall I deny you? No: farewell, my lord.

OTHELLO
Farewell, my Desdemona.

DESDEMONA
Emilia, come.

Exit EMILIA and DESDEMONA.

OTHELLO
Excellent wretch! Perdition catch my soul,
But I do love thee! and when I love thee not,
Chaos is come again.

Joins IAGO in a game of pool.

IAGO
Othello?

OTHELLO
Iago?

IAGO
Did Michael Cassio, when you woo'd my lady,
Know of your love?

OTHELLO
He did, from first to last: why dost thou ask?

IAGO
But for a satisfaction of my thought;
No further harm.

OTHELLO
Why of thy thought, Iago?

IAGO
I did not think he had been acquainted with her.

OTHELLO
O, yes; and went between us very oft.

IAGO
Indeed!

OTHELLO
Indeed! Ay, indeed: discern'st thou aught in that?
Is he not honest?

IAGO
Honest, my lord!

OTHELLO
Honest! Ay, honest.

IAGO
My lord, for aught I know.

OTHELLO
What dost thou think?

IAGO
Think, my lord!

OTHELLO
Think, my lord!
By heaven, he echoes me,
As if there were some monster in his thought
Too hideous to be shown. Thou dost mean something:
I heard thee say even now, thou likedst not that,
When Cassio left my wife:
And when I told thee he was of my counsel
In my whole course of wooing, thou criedst 'Indeed?'
And didst contract and purse thy brow together
If thou dost love me,
Show me thy thought.

IAGO
My lord, you know I love you.

OTHELLO
I think thou dost;

IAGO
For Michael Cassio,
I dare be sworn I think that he is honest.

OTHELLO
I think so too.

IAGO
Men should be what they seem;
Or those that be not, would they might seem none!

OTHELLO
Certain, men should be what they seem.

IAGO
Why, then, I think Cassio's an honest man.

OTHELLO
Nay, yet there's more in this:
I prithee speak to me, as to thy thinkings,
As thou dost ruminate, and give thy worst of thoughts
The worst of words.

IAGO
Good my lord. Why say they are vile and false?

OTHELLO
Thou dost conspire against thy friend, Iago,
If thou but think'st him wrong'd and makest his ear
A stranger to thy thoughts.

IAGO
Perchance I am vicious in my guess
As I confess it is my nature's plague
To spy into abuses, and shapes faults that are not
It were not for your quiet or your good to let you know my thoughts.

OTHELLO
What dost thou mean?

IAGO
Good name in man and woman, dear my lord,

Is the immediate jewel of their souls:
Who steals my purse steals trash; 'tis something, nothing;
'Twas mine, 'tis his, and has been slave to thousands:
But he that filches from me my good name
Robs me of that which not enriches him
And makes me poor indeed.

OTHELLO
By heaven, I'll know thy thoughts.

IAGO
You cannot, if my heart were in your hand;
Nor shall not, whilst 'tis in my custody.

OTHELLO
Ha!

IAGO
O, beware, my lord, of jealousy;
It is the green-eyed monster which doth mock
The meat it feeds on; that cuckold lives in bliss
Who, certain of his fate, loves not his wronger;
But, O, what damned minutes tells he o'er
Who dotes, yet doubts, suspects, yet strongly loves!
Good heaven, the souls of all my tribe defend
From jealousy!

OTHELLO
Why, why is this?
Think'st thou I'd make a life of jealousy,
To follow still the changes of the moon
With fresh suspicions? No, Iago;
I'll see before I doubt; when I doubt, prove;
And on the proof, there is no more but this –
Away at once with love or jealousy!

IAGO
I am glad of it; for now I shall have reason
To show the love and duty that I bear you
With franker spirit: therefore, as I am bound,
Receive it from me. I speak not yet of proof.
Look to your wife; observe her well with Cassio;
Wear your eye thus, not jealous nor secure:

I would not have your free and noble nature,
Out of self-bounty, be abused; look to't:
She did deceive her father, marrying you;
And when she seem'd to shake and fear your looks,
She loved them most.

OTHELLO
And so she did.

IAGO
Why, go to then;
She that, so young, could give out such a seeming,
To seal her father's eyes up close as oak –
He thought 'twas witchcraft – but I am much to blame;
I humbly do beseech you of your pardon
For too much loving you…
I see this hath a little dash'd your spirits.

OTHELLO
Not a jot, not a jot.

IAGO
I' faith, I fear it has.
I hope you will consider what is spoke
Comes from my love. Cassio's my worthy friend –
My lord, I see you're moved.

OTHELLO
No, not much moved:
I do not think but Desdemona's honest.

IAGO
Long live she so! And long live you to think so!

OTHELLO
And yet, how nature erring from itself –

IAGO
Ay, there's the point: as – to be bold with you –
Not to affect many proposed matches
Of her own clime, complexion, and degree,
Whereto we see in all things nature tends –
Foh! one may smell in such a will most rank,
Foul disproportion thoughts unnatural.

But pardon me; I do not in position
Distinctly speak of her; though I may fear
Her will, recoiling to her better judgment,
May fall to match you with her country forms
And happily repent.

OTHELLO

If more thou dost perceive, let me know more;
Set on thy wife to observe:

IAGO

(*Going.*) My lord, I take my leave.

IAGO, taking empties back to the bar, decides to turn back.

Othello, I would I might entreat your honour
To scan this thing no further; leave it to time:
Though it be fit that Cassio have his place,
For sure, he fills it up with great ability,
Yet, if you please to hold him off awhile,
You shall by that perceive him and his means:
Note, if your lady strain his entertainment
With any strong or vehement importunity;
Much will be seen in that. In the mean time,
Let me be thought too busy in my fears –
As worthy cause I have to fear I am –
And hold her free, I do beseech your honour.

Exit.

OTHELLO

This fellow's of exceeding honesty,
And knows all qualities, with a learned spirit,
Of human dealings. If I do prove her haggard,
Though that her jesses were my dear heartstrings,
I'd whistle her off and let her down the wind,
To pray at fortune. Haply, for I am black
And have not those soft parts of conversation
That chamberers have, or for I am declined
Into the vale of years – yet that's not much –
She's gone. I am abused; and my relief
Must be to loathe her. O curse of marriage,
That we can call these delicate creatures ours,

And not their appetites! I had rather be a toad,
And live upon the vapour of a dungeon,
Than keep a corner in the thing I love
For others' uses. Yet, 'tis the plague of great ones;
Prerogatived are they less than the base;
'Tis destiny unshunnable, like death:
Even then this forked plague is fated to us
When we do quicken.

Re-enter DESDEMONA and EMILIA.

Look
If she be false, O then heaven mocks itself
I'll not believe't.

DESDEMONA
How now, my dear Othello!

OTHELLO
I am to blame.

DESDEMONA
Why do you speak so faintly?
Are you not well?

OTHELLO
I have a pain upon my forehead here.

DESDEMONA
'Faith, that's with drinking; 'twill away again:
Let me but kiss it hard, within this hour
It will be well.

She puts the handkerchief around his neck. It falls to the ground.

OTHELLO
Come, go in with me.

DESDEMONA
I am very sorry that you are not well.

OTHELLO and DESDEMONA exit leaving EMILIA. She picks up the handkerchief.

Re-enter IAGO.

IAGO
How now! What do you here alone?

EMILIA
I have a thing for you.

IAGO
You have a thing for me?
It is a common thing –

EMILIA
Ha!

IAGO
To have a foolish wife.

EMILIA
O, is that all? What will you give me now?

EMILIA tries to kiss IAGO. He spots the handkerchief.

IAGO
Hast stol'n it from her?

EMILIA
No, 'faith; she let it drop by negligence.

IAGO
Give it me!

EMILIA
What will you do with 't?

IAGO
(*Snatching it.*) Why, what's that to you?

EMILIA
If it be not for some purpose of import,
Give't me again: poor lady, she'll run mad
When she shall lack it.

IAGO
I have use for it.

Exit EMILIA.

I will on Cassio's person place this napkin,
And let him find it.

This may do something.

Re-enter OTHELLO.

OTHELLO
Iago! False to me?

IAGO
Why, how now, general!

OTHELLO
Thou hast set me on the rack:
I swear 'tis better to be much abused
Than but to know't a little.

IAGO
How now, my lord!

OTHELLO
What sense had I of her stol'n hours of lust?
I saw't not, thought it not, it harm'd not me:
I slept the next night well, was free and merry;
I found not Cassio's kisses on her lips:
He that is robb'd, not wanting what is stol'n,
Let him not know't, and he's not robb'd at all.

IAGO
I am sorry to hear this.

OTHELLO
I had been happy, if the general camp,
Pioners and all, had tasted her sweet body,
So I had nothing known. O, now, for ever
Farewell the tranquil mind! Farewell content!

IAGO
Is't possible, my lord?

OTHELLO
Villain, be sure thou prove my love a whore,
Be sure of it; give me the ocular proof:
Or by the worth of man's eternal soul,
Thou hadst been better have been born a dog
Than answer my waked wrath!

IAGO

Is't come to this?

OTHELLO

Make me to see't; or, at the least, so prove it,
That the probation bear no hinge nor loop
To hang a doubt on; or woe upon thy life!

IAGO

My noble lord –

OTHELLO

If thou dost slander her and torture me,
Never pray more; abandon all remorse;
On horror's head horrors accumulate;
Do deeds to make heaven weep, all earth amazed;
For nothing canst thou to damnation add
Greater than that.

IAGO

O monstrous world! Take note, take note, O world,
To be direct and honest is not safe.
I thank you for this profit; and from hence
I'll love no friend, sith love breeds such offence.

OTHELLO

Nay, stay: thou shouldst be honest.

IAGO

I should be wise, for honesty's a fool
And loses that it works for.

OTHELLO

By the world,
I think my girl be honest and think she is not;
I think that thou art just and think thou art not.
I'll have some proof. Her name, that was as fresh
As Dian's visage, is now begrimed and black
As mine own face. Would I were satisfied!

IAGO

How satisfied, my lord?
Would you, the supervisor, grossly gape on?
Behold her topp'd?

What then? How then?
What shall I say? Where's satisfaction?
It is impossible you should see this,
Were they as prime as goats, as hot as monkeys,
and fools as gross
As ignorance made drunk.

OTHELLO
Give me a living reason she's disloyal.

IAGO
I do not like the office:
But, sith I am enter'd in this cause so far,
Prick'd to't by foolish honesty and love,
I will go on. Tell me but this,
Have you not sometimes seen a handkerchief
Spotted with strawberries in your wife's hand?

OTHELLO
I gave her such a one; 'twas my first gift.

IAGO
I know not that; but such a handkerchief –
I am sure it was your wife's – did I today
See Cassio wipe his beard with.

OTHELLO
If it be that –

IAGO
If it be that, or any that was hers,
It speaks against her.

OTHELLO
O, that the slave had forty thousand lives!
One is too poor, too weak for my revenge.
Now do I see 'tis true. Look here, Iago;
All my fond love thus do I blow to heaven.
'Tis gone.
Arise, black vengeance, from thy hollow hell!
Yield up, O love, thy crown and hearted throne
To tyrannous hate! Swell, bosom, with thy fraught,
For 'tis of aspics' tongues!

IAGO
Yet be content.

OTHELLO
O, blood, blood, blood!

IAGO
Patience, I say; your mind perhaps may change.

OTHELLO
Never, Iago: my bloody thoughts, with violent pace,
Shall ne'er look back, ne'er ebb to humble love,
Till that a capable and wide revenge
Swallow them up.

IAGO
Witness that here Iago doth give up
The execution of his wit, hands, heart,
To wrong'd Othello's service! Let him command,
And to obey shall be in me remorse,
What bloody business ever.

OTHELLO
Within these three days let me hear thee say
That Cassio's not alive.

IAGO
My friend is dead; 'tis done at your request:
But let her live.

OTHELLO
Damn her, lewd minx! O, damn her!
To furnish me with some swift means of death
For the fair devil. Now art thou my lieutenant.

IAGO
I am your own for ever.

Pub Moment. IAGO plants the handkerchief in CASSIO's coat.

DESDEMONA
Where should I lose that handkerchief, Emilia?

EMILIA
I know not, madam.

DESDEMONA
Believe me, I had rather have lost my purse
Full of crusadoes: and, but my noble Moor
Is true of mind and made of no such baseness
As jealous creatures are, it were enough
To put him to ill thinking.

EMILIA
Is he not jealous?

DESDEMONA
Who, he? I think the sun where he was born
Drew all such humours from him.
I will not leave him now till Cassio
Be call'd to him.

Enter OTHELLO.

How is't with you, my lord?

OTHELLO
Well, my good lady.
How do you, Desdemona?

DESDEMONA
Well, my good lord.

OTHELLO
Give me your hand: this hand is moist, my lady.

DESDEMONA
It yet hath felt no age nor known no sorrow.

OTHELLO
'Tis a good hand,
A frank one.

DESDEMONA
You may, indeed, say so;
For 'twas that hand that gave away my heart.
Come now, your promise.

OTHELLO
What promise, chuck?

DESDEMONA
I have sent to bid Cassio come speak with you.

OTHELLO
Where is thy handkerchief?

DESDEMONA
I have it not about me.

OTHELLO
Not?

DESDEMONA
No, indeed, my lord.

OTHELLO
That is a fault.
To lose't or give't away were such perdition
As nothing else could match.

DESDEMONA
Is't possible?

OTHELLO
Most veritable; therefore look to't well.

DESDEMONA
Then would to God that I had never seen't!

OTHELLO
Ha! wherefore?

DESDEMONA
Why do you speak so startingly and rash?

OTHELLO
Is't lost? is't gone? speak, is it out
O' the way?

DESDEMONA
Heaven bless us!

OTHELLO
Say you?

DESDEMONA
It is not lost; but what an if it were?

OTHELLO
How!

DESDEMONA
I say, it is not lost.

OTHELLO
Fetch't, let me see't.

DESDEMONA
Why, so I can, sir, but I will not now.
This is a trick to put me from my suit:
Pray you, let Cassio be received again.

OTHELLO
Fetch me the handkerchief: my mind misgives.

DESDEMONA
Come, come;
You'll never meet a more sufficient man.

OTHELLO
The handkerchief!

DESDEMONA
I pray, talk me of Cassio.

OTHELLO
The handkerchief!

DESDEMONA
A man that all his time
Hath founded his good fortunes on your love,
Shared dangers with you –

OTHELLO
The handkerchief!

DESDEMONA
In sooth, you are to blame.

OTHELLO
Away!

OTHELLO exits.

EMILIA
Is not this man jealous?

DESDEMONA
I ne'er saw this before.

EMILIA
'Tis not a year or two shows us a man:
They are all but stomachs, and we all but food;
To eat us hungerly, and when they are full,
They belch us.

DESDEMONA
Alas the day! I never gave him cause.

EMILIA
But jealous souls will not be answer'd so;
They are not ever jealous for the cause,
But jealous for they are jealous: 'tis a monster
Begot upon itself, born on itself.

DESDEMONA
Heaven keep that monster from Othello's mind!

EMILIA
Lady, amen.
Look you, Cassio and my husband!

Enter CASSIO and IAGO.

We witness CASSIO and DESDEMONA chatting. EMILIA drags IAGO off into a corner. They appear to be arguing. EMILIA, enraged, exits. IAGO makes sure CASSIO has his coat and then follows. DESDEMONA leaves CASSIO when they finish chatting. When he is alone he puts his coat on and finds the hankerchief.

Enter BIANCA.

BIANCA
Save you, friend Cassio!

CASSIO
How is it with you, my most fair Bianca?

BIANCA
What, keep a week away? Seven days and nights?

Eight score eight hours? And lovers' absent hours,
More tedious than the dial eight score times?
O weary reckoning!

CASSIO

Pardon me, Bianca:
I have this while with leaden thoughts been press'd:
But I shall, in a more continuate time,
Strike off this score of absence.

He tries to give the handkerchief to BIANCA.

BIANCA

O Cassio, whence came this?
This is some token from a newer friend:
To the felt absence now I feel a cause:
Is't come to this? Well, well.

CASSIO

Go to, woman!
Throw your vile guesses in the devil's teeth,
From whence you have them. You are jealous now
That this is from some mistress, some remembrance:
No, in good troth, Bianca.

BIANCA

Why, whose is it?

CASSIO

I know not, sweet: I found it
Take it, and leave me for this time.

BIANCA

Leave you! Wherefore?

CASSIO

I do attend here on the general;
And think it no addition, nor my wish,
To have him see me woman'd.

BIANCA

Why, I pray you?

CASSIO

Not that I love you not.

BIANCA

But that you do not love me.
I pray you, bring me on the way a little,
And say if I shall see you soon at night.

CASSIO

'Tis but a little way that I can bring you;
For I attend here: but I'll see you soon.

They have a kiss. Bit of a fondle. Promise of more to come.

BIANCA

'Tis very good;

BIANCA exits. CASSIO nervously plays with his baseball cap. IAGO enters and sends CASSIO to the bar to get drinks.

IAGO

My noble lord
Whilst you were gone
Cassio came hither: I shifted him away,
Bade him anon return and here speak with me;
The which he promised. Do but encave yourself,
And mark the fleers, the gibes, and notable scorns,
That dwell in every region of his face;
For I will make him tell the tale anew,
Where, how, how oft, how long ago, and when
He hath, and is again to cope your wife:
I say, but mark his gesture.

OTHELLO

Dost thou hear, Iago?
I will be found most cunning in my patience;
But – dost thou hear? – most bloody.

OTHELLO retires.

Re-enter CASSIO.

IAGO

How do you now, lieutenant?

CASSIO

The worser that you give me the addition
Whose want even kills me.

IAGO
Ply Desdemona well, and you are sure on't.

Speaking lower.

Now, if this suit lay in Bianca's power,
How quickly should you speed!

CASSIO
Alas, poor caitiff!

IAGO
I never knew a woman love man so.

CASSIO
Alas poor rogue, I think I'faith she loves me.

IAGO
She gives it out that you shall marry her.

CASSIO
I marry her!
Prithee bare some charity to my wit.
Do not think its so unwholesome.
She is persuaded I will marry her,
out of her own love and
flattery, not out of my promise.
She haunts me in every place.
I was the other day talking on the bank
and thither comes the bauble,
and, by this hand, she falls me thus about my neck –
Crying 'O Cassio!'
So hangs, and lolls, and weeps upon me; so hales,
and pulls me: ha, ha, ha!

Enter BIANCA.

BIANCA
Cassio!

CASSIO
What do you mean by this haunting of me?

BIANCA
Let the devil and his dam haunt you!

What did you mean by that same handkerchief you gave me even now?
I was a fine fool to take it.
A likely piece of work, that you should find
on your person, and not know who left it there!
This is some minx's token,
There give it your hobby-horse; wheresoever you had it.

CASSIO

How now, my sweet Bianca! How now! How now!

BIANCA

If you'll come to supper tonight, you may; if you will not,
come when you are next prepared for.

Exit BIANCA.

IAGO

After her, after her.

Exit CASSIO.

OTHELLO

How shall I murder him, Iago?

IAGO

Did you perceive how he laughed at his vice?
And did you see the handkerchief?

OTHELLO

Was that mine?

IAGO

Yours. Desdemona gave it him, and he
hath given it his whore.

OTHELLO

I would have him nine years a-killing.
A fine woman, a fair woman, a sweet woman.

IAGO

Nay, you must forget that.

OTHELLO

Ay, let her rot, and perish, and be damned tonight;
for she shall not live: no, my heart is turned to

stone; I strike it, and it hurts my hand.
O the world has not a sweeter creature.

IAGO
Nay, that's not your way.

OTHELLO
Hang her! I do but say what she is: so delicate with her needle: an admirable musician: O! she will sing the savageness out of a bear: of so high and plenteous wit and invention: –

IAGO
She's the worse for all this.

OTHELLO
O, a thousand thousand times: and then, of so gentle a condition!

IAGO
Ay, too gentle.

OTHELLO
Nay, that's certain: but yet the pity of it, Iago!
O Iago, the pity of it, Iago!

IAGO
If you are so fond over her iniquity, give her patent to offend; for, if it touch not you, it comes near nobody.

OTHELLO
I will chop her into messes: cuckold me!
With mine officer!

Enter DESDEMONA and LODOVICO.

DESDEMONA
Cousin, there's fall'n between him and my lord
An unkind breach, but you shall make it all well.

LODOVICO
Is there division 'twixt my lord and Cassio?

DESDEMONA
A most unhappy one: I would do much

To atone them, for the love I bear to Cassio.

OTHELLO
(*Striking her.*) Devil!

DESDEMONA
I have not deserved this.

LODOVICO
Make her amends.

DESDEMONA
I will not stay to offend you. (*Going.*)

LODOVICO
Call her back…

OTHELLO
Mistress!

DESDEMONA stops.

What would you with her, sir?
You that did wish that I would make her turn:
Sir, she can turn, and turn, and yet go on,
And turn again; and she can weep, sir, weep;
Proceed you in your tears.

LODOVICO
(*Challenging OTHELLO.*)
Is this the noble Moor
Whom passion could not shake? Whose solid virtue
The shot of accident, nor dart of chance,
Could neither graze nor pierce?
Are his wits safe? Is he not light of brain?

OTHELLO turns, grabs EMILIA and drags her away.

OTHELLO
You have seen nothing then?

EMILIA
Nor ever heard, nor ever did suspect.

OTHELLO
Yes, you have seen Cassio and she together.

EMILIA
But then I saw no harm, and then I heard
Each syllable that breath made up between them.

OTHELLO
What, did they never whisper?

EMILIA
Never, my lord.

OTHELLO
Nor send you out o' the way?

EMILIA
Never.

OTHELLO turns on DESDEMONA.

OTHELLO
Pray, chuck, come hither.
Let me see your eyes.

DESDEMONA
What horrible fancy's this?

OTHELLO
Why, what art thou?

DESDEMONA
Your wife, my lord; your true
And loyal wife.

OTHELLO
Come swear it. Swear thou art honest.

DESDEMONA
Heaven dost truly know it.

OTHELLO
Heaven truly knows that thou art false as hell.

DESDEMONA
To whom, my lord? With whom? How am I false?

OTHELLO
Ah Desdemona! Away, away, away!

DESDEMONA

Alas the heavy day, why do you weep?
Am I the motive of these tears, my lord?

DESDEMONA clears the pool room. She and OTHELLO are alone.

OTHELLO

Had it pleased heaven
To try me with affliction; had they rain'd
All kinds of sores and shames on my bare head.
Steep'd me in poverty to the very lips,
Given to captivity me and my utmost hopes,
I should have found in some place of my soul
A drop of patience: but, alas, to make me
A fixed figure for the time of scorn
To point his slow unmoving finger at!
Yet could I bear that too; well, very well:
But there, where I have garner'd up my heart,
Where either I must live, or bear no life;
The fountain from the which my current runs,
Or else dries up; to be discarded thence!
Or keep it as a cistern for foul toads
To knot and gender in!

DESDEMONA

I hope my noble lord esteems me honest.

OTHELLO

O, ay; as summer flies are in the shambles,
That quicken even with blowing. O thou weed,
Who art so lovely fair and smell'st so sweet
That the sense aches at thee, would thou hadst
ne'er been born!

DESDEMONA

Alas, what ignorant sin have I committed?

OTHELLO

Was this fair paper, this most goodly book,
Made to write 'whore' upon? What committed!
Committed! O thou public commoner!
I should make very forges of my cheeks,
That would to cinders burn up modesty,

Did I but speak thy deeds. What committed!
Heaven stops the nose at it and the moon winks,
The bawdy wind that kisses all it meets
Is hush'd within the hollow mine of earth,
And will not hear it. What committed!
Impudent strumpet!

DESDEMONA
By heaven, you do me wrong.

OTHELLO
Are you not a strumpet?

DESDEMONA
No.
If to preserve this vessel for my lord
From any other foul unlawful touch
Be not to be a strumpet, I am none.

OTHELLO
What, not a whore?

DESDEMONA
No, as I shall be saved.

OTHELLO
Is't possible?

DESDEMONA
O, heaven forgive us!

OTHELLO
I cry you mercy, then:
I took you for that cunning whore
That married with Othello.

OTHELLO exits through fire exit.

EMILA enters.

EMILIA
How do you, madam? how do you, my good lady?

DESDEMONA
'Faith, half asleep.
I cannot weep; nor answer have I none

The walls open to reveal OTHELLO outside. IAGO joins him.

OTHELLO
Get me some poison, Iago; this night: I'll not expostulate with her, lest her body and beauty unprovide my mind again: this night, Iago.

IAGO
Do it not with poison, strangle her in her bed, even the bed she hath contaminated.

OTHELLO
Good, good: the justice of it pleases: very good.

IAGO
And for Cassio, let me be his undertaker.

OTHELLO
Excellent good.

IAGO moves into the pub, the walls closing behind him.

IAGO
Madam, how is't with you?

DESDEMONA
Am I that name, Iago?

IAGO
What name, fair lady?

DESDEMONA
Such as she says my lord did say I was.

EMILIA
He call'd her whore: a beggar in his drink
Could not have laid such terms upon his callat.

IAGO
Why did he so?

DESDEMONA
I do not know; I am sure I am none such.

EMILIA
How comes this trick upon him?

DESDEMONA
Nay, heaven doth know.

EMILIA
I will be hang'd, if some eternal villain,
Some busy and insinuating rogue,
Some cogging, cozening slave, to get some office,
Have not devised this slander; I'll be hang'd else.

DESDEMONA
If any such there be, heaven pardon him!

EMILIA
A halter pardon him! and hell gnaw his bones!
Why should he call her whore? who keeps her company?
What place? What time? What form? What likelihood?
The Moor's abused by some most villanous knave,
Some base notorious knave, some scurvy fellow.
O heaven, that such companions thou'dst unfold,
And put in every honest hand a whip
To lash the rascal naked through the world.

IAGO
Speak within doors.

EMILIA
O, fie upon them! Some such squire he was
That turn'd your wit the seamy side without,
And made you to suspect me with the Moor.

IAGO
You are a fool: go to.

DESDEMONA
O good Iago,
What shall I do to win my lord again?
Good friend, go to him; for, by this light of heaven,
I know not how I lost him.

OTHELLO shouts into the pub.

OTHELLO
Desdemona – get you gone…dismiss your attendant there : look it be done.

DESDEMONA signifies no intention of following his demand, pulls EMILIA into the toilets.

Enter RODERIGO.

IAGO

How now, Roderigo!

RODERIGO

I do not find that thou dealest justly with me.

IAGO

What in the contrary?

RODERIGO

Every day thou daffest me with some device.
I have wasted myself out of
my means. The jewels you have had from me to
deliver Desdemona would half have corrupted a
votarist: you have told me she hath received you
and returned me expectations and comforts of sudden
respect and acquaintance, but I find none.

IAGO

Well; go to; very well.

RODERIGO

Very well! Go to! I cannot go to, man; nor 'tis
not very well: nay, I think it is scurvy, and begin
to find myself fobbed in it.

IAGO

Very well.

RODERIGO

I tell you 'tis not very well. I will make you
known to Desdemona.

IAGO

Why, now I see there's mettle in thee, and even from
this instant do build on thee a better opinion than
ever before. Give me thy hand, Roderigo: thou hast
taken against me a most just exception; but yet, I
protest, I have dealt most directly in thy affair.

RODERIGO
It hath not appeared.

IAGO
I grant indeed it hath not appeared, and your suspicion is not without wit and judgment. But, Roderigo, if thou hast that in thee indeed, which I have greater reason to believe now than ever, I mean purpose, courage and valour, this night show it: if thou the next night following enjoy not Desdemona, take me from this world.

RODERIGO
Well, what is it? Is it within reason and compass?

IAGO
The removing of Cassio.

RODERIGO
How do you mean, removing of him?

IAGO
By knocking out his brains.

RODERIGO
And that you would have me to do?

IAGO
Aye, if you dare do yourself a profit and a right
I will be near to second your attempt, and he shall fall
Between us.

DESDEMONA and EMILIA in the women's toilet.

EMILIA
I would you had never seen him!
This Lodovico is a proper man.
A very handsome man.

DESDEMONA
He speaks well.

EMILIA
I know a lady who would have walked barefoot
to Mecca for a touch of his nether lip.

DESDEMONA

My eyes do itch;
Doth that bode weeping?
O, these men, these men!
Dost thou in conscience think – tell me Emilia –
That there be women do abuse their husbands
In such gross kind?

EMILIA

There be some such, no question.

DESDEMONA

Wouldst thou do such a deed for all the world?

EMILIA

Why, would not you?

DESDEMONA

No, by this heavenly light!

EMILIA

Nor I neither by this heavenly light;
I might do't as well i' the dark.

DESDEMONA

Wouldst thou do such a deed for all the world?

EMILIA

The world's a huge thing: it is a great price.
For a small vice.

DESDEMONA

In troth, I think thou wouldst not.

EMILIA

In troth, I think I should; and undo't when I had done. Marry, I would not do such a thing for a joint-ring, nor for measures of lawn, nor for gowns, petticoats, nor caps, nor any petty exhibition; but for the whole world – why who would not make her husband a cuckold to make him a monarch? I should venture purgatory for't.

DESDEMONA

Beshrew me, if I would do such a wrong

For the whole world.

EMILIA

Why the wrong is but a wrong i' the world: and having the world for your labour, 'tis a wrong in your own world, and you might quickly make it right.

DESDEMONA

I do not think there is any such woman.

EMILIA

Yes, a dozen, and as many to th'vantage as would
Store the world they played for.
But I do think it is their husbands' faults
If wives do fall: say that they slack their duties,
And pour our treasures into foreign laps,
Or else break out in peevish jealousies
Throwing restraint upon us; or say they strike us,
Or scant our former having in despite,
Why, we have galls: and though we have some grace
Yet have we some revenge. Let husbands know
Their wives have sense like them: they see, and smell,
And have palates both for sweet and sour
As husbands have. What is it that they do
When they change us for others? Is it sport?
I think it is: and doth affection breed it?
I think it doth: is't frailty that thus errs?
It is so too: and have not we affections?
Desires for sport, and frailty, as men have?
Then let them use us well: else let them know,
The ills we do, their ills instruct us so.

EMILIA and DESDEMONA say their farewells and EMILIA exits.

Outside.

RODERIGO

Be near at hand; I may miscarry in't.
I have no great devotion to the deed;

IAGO

It makes us or mars us. Think on that.

RODERIGO goes to prepare for the attack.

Now, whether he kill Cassio or Cassio him,
Or each do kill the other.
Every way makes my gain.

CASSIO and BIANCA walk through the car park. RODERIGO attacks CASSIO. CASSIO fights back. IAGO runs on and attacks CASSIO and exits. CASSIO and RODERIGO are on the floor. BIANCA is screaming.

BIANCA
Help, ho!

CASSIO
O, help, ho! light!

Inside the pub.

OTHELLO
'Tis he: – O brave Iago, honest and just,
That hast such noble sense of thy friend's wrong!
Thou teachest me. Minion, your dear lies dead,
And your unblest fate hies: strumpet, I come.

Outside.

CASSIO
O, help!

RODERIGO
O wretched villain!

Re-enter IAGO, with a light.

IAGO
Who's there?

CASSIO
Here, here! For heaven's sake, help me!

IAGO
What's the matter?
What are you here that cry so grievously?

CASSIO
Iago? O, I am spoil'd, undone by villains!

BIANCA
Give him some help.

IAGO
O me, lieutenant! What villains have done this?

CASSIO
I think that one of them is hereabout,
And cannot make away.

IAGO
O treacherous villains!
What are you there? Come and give some help.

Enter LODOVICO and MONTANO.

RODERIGO
O, help me here!

CASSIO
That's one of them.

IAGO
O murderous slave! O villain!

Attacks RODERIGO.

RODERIGO
O, Damned Iago! O Inhuman dog!

IAGO
Signior Lodovico?
Here's Cassio hurt by villains.

MONTANO
Cassio!

LODOVICO
How is't, brother!

CASSIO
My leg …

BIANCA
O my dear Cassio! My sweet Cassio! O Cassio,
Cassio, Cassio!

IAGO

O notable strumpet! Cassio, may you suspect
Who they should be that have thus mangled you?

CASSIO

No.

BIANCA

O Cassio, Cassio, Cassio!

IAGO

Gentlemen all, I do suspect this trash
To be a party in this injury.
Patience awhile, good Cassio. Come, come;
Lend me a light. Know we this face or no?
Alas my friend and my dear countryman
Roderigo! no: – yes, sure: O heaven! Roderigo.

To BIANCA.

For you, mistress,
Save you your labour. He that lies slain
here, Cassio,
Was my dear friend: what malice was between you?

CASSIO

None in the world.

IAGO

(*To BIANCA.*)
Look you pale, mistress?
Do you perceive the gastness of her eye?
Behold her well; I pray you, look upon her:
Do you see, gentlemen? Nay, guiltiness will speak,
Though tongues were out of use.

Enter EMILIA.

EMILIA

What's the matter, husband?

IAGO

Cassio hath here been set on in the dark
By Roderigo and fellows that are scaped:
He's almost slain, and Roderigo gone.

This is the fruit of whoring. Prithee, Emilia,
Go know of Cassio where he supp'd tonight.

To BIANCA.

What, do you shake at that?

BIANCA
He supp'd at my house; but I therefore shake not.

IAGO
O, did he so?

EMILIA
Fie, fie upon thee, strumpet!

BIANCA
I am no strumpet; but of life as honest
As you that thus abuse me.

EMILIA
As I! Foh! Fie upon thee!

IAGO
Kind gentlemen, let's go see poor Cassio dress'd.
Come, mistress, you must tell's another tale.
Emilia run you to the Cypress
And tell my lord and lady what hath happ'd.
Will you go on? I pray.
(*Aside.*) This is the night
That either makes me or fordoes me quite.

Exit. Walls close.

OTHELLO is in the pub.

OTHELLO
It is the cause, it is the cause, my soul –
Let me not name it to you, you chaste stars!
It is the cause. Yet I'll not shed her blood;
Nor scar that whiter skin of hers than snow,
And smooth as monumental alabaster.
Yet she must die, else she'll betray more men.
Put out the light, and then put out the light:
If I quench thee, thou flaming minister,
I can again thy former light restore,

Should I repent me: but once put out thy light,
Thou cunning'st pattern of excelling nature,
I know not where is that Promethean heat
That can thy light relume.

DESDEMONA
Who's there? Othello?

OTHELLO
Ay. Have you pray'd tonight, Desdemona?

DESDEMONA
Ay, my lord.

OTHELLO grabs DESDEMONA and drags her to pool table.

OTHELLO
If you bethink yourself of any crime
Unreconciled as yet to heaven and grace,
Solicit for it straight.

DESDEMONA
Alas, my lord, what do you mean by that?

OTHELLO
Well, do it, and be brief; I will walk by:
I would not kill thy unprepared spirit;
No; heaven forfend! I would not kill thy soul.

DESDEMONA
Talk you of killing?

OTHELLO
Ay, I do.

DESDEMONA
Then heaven
Have mercy on me!

OTHELLO
Amen, with all my heart!

DESDEMONA
If you say so, I hope you will not kill me.
And yet I fear you
why I should fear I know not,

Since guiltiness I know not; but yet I feel I fear.

OTHELLO
Think on thy sins.

DESDEMONA
They are loves I bear to you.

OTHELLO
Ay, and for that thou diest.

DESDEMONA
That death's unnatural that kills for loving.

OTHELLO
That handkerchief which I so loved and gave thee
Thou gavest to Cassio.

DESDEMONA
No, by my life and soul!
Send for the man, and ask him.

OTHELLO
Thou art on thy deathbed.

DESDEMONA
Ay? But not yet to die
I never did
Offend you in my life; never loved Cassio
But with such general warranty of heaven
As I might love: I never gave him token.

OTHELLO
By heaven, I saw my handkerchief in's hand.
O perjured woman! Thou dost stone my heart,
And makest me call what I intend to do
A murder, which I thought a sacrifice:
I saw the handkerchief.

DESDEMONA
He found it then;
I never gave it him: send for him hither;
Let him confess a truth.

OTHELLO
He hath confess'd.

DESDEMONA
What, my lord?

OTHELLO
That he hath used thee.

DESDEMONA
How? unlawfully?

OTHELLO
Ay.

DESDEMONA
He will not say so.

OTHELLO
No, his mouth is stopp'd;
Honest Iago hath ta'en order for't.

DESDEMONA
O! My fear interprets: what, is he dead?

OTHELLO
Had all his hairs been lives, my great revenge
Had stomach for them all.

DESDEMONA
Alas! He is betray'd and I undone.

OTHELLO
Out, strumpet! weep'st thou for him to my face? (*He strikes her. They fight. Eventually he subdues her upon the pool table.*)

DESDEMONA
O, banish me, my lord, but kill me not!

OTHELLO
Down, strumpet! (*He strangles her.*)
Cold, cold my girl!
Even like thy chastity. O cursed slave!
Whip me, ye devils,
From the possession of this heavenly sight!
Blow me about in winds! Roast me in sulphur!
Wash me in steep-down gulfs of liquid fire!
O Desdemona! Desdemona! Dead!

EMILIA is outside the pub and is trying to get in. She shouts through the windows. She bangs on the fire exit door.

EMILIA

What, ho! My lord, my lord?
O, good my lord, I would speak a word with you!
I do beseech you
That I may speak with you, O, good my lord!

OTHELLO unlocks the door.

Enter EMILIA.

OTHELLO

What, now?

EMILIA

Cassio, my lord, hath kill'd Roderigo.

OTHELLO

Roderigo kill'd!
And Cassio kill'd!

EMILIA

No, Cassio is not kill'd.

OTHELLO

Not Cassio kill'd! Then murder's out of tune,
And sweet revenge grows harsh.

DESDEMONA makes a noise.

EMILIA

Alas, what cry is that?

OTHELLO

That! What?

EMILIA

Out, and alas! that was my lady's voice.
Help! Help, ho! Help! O lady, speak again!
Sweet Desdemona! O sweet mistress, speak!

DESDEMONA

A guiltless death I die.

EMILIA
O, who hath done this deed?

DESDEMONA
Nobody; I myself. Farewell.
Commend me to my kind lord:

She dies.

OTHELLO
You heard her say herself, it was not I.

EMILIA
She said so: I must needs report the truth.

OTHELLO
She's, like a liar, gone to burning hell:
'Twas I that kill'd her.

EMILIA
O, the more angel she,
And you the blacker devil!

OTHELLO
She turn'd to folly, and she was a whore.

EMILIA
Thou dost belie her, and thou art a devil.

OTHELLO
She was false as water.

EMILIA
Thou art rash as fire, to say
That she was false: O, she was heavenly true!

OTHELLO
Cassio did top her; ask thy husband else.
O, I were damn'd beneath all depth in hell,
But that I did proceed upon just grounds
To this extremity. Thy husband knew it all.

EMILIA
That she was false to wedlock?

OTHELLO
Ay, with Cassio. Nay, had she been true,

If heaven would make me such another world
Of one entire and perfect chrysolite,
I'd not have sold her for it.

EMILIA
My husband!

OTHELLO
Ay, 'twas he that told me first:
An honest man he is, and hates the slime
That sticks on filthy deeds.

EMILIA
O mistress, villany hath made mocks with love,
My husband say that she was false!

OTHELLO
He, woman;
I say thy husband: dost understand the word?
My friend, thy husband, honest, honest Iago.

EMILIA
If he say so, may his pernicious soul
Rot half a grain a day! He lies to the heart:
She was too fond of her most filthy bargain.

OTHELLO
Ha!

EMILIA
Do thy worst:
This deed of thine is no more worthy heaven
Than thou wast worthy her.

OTHELLO
Peace, you were best.

EMILIA
Thou hast not half that power to do me harm
As I have to be hurt. O gull! O dolt!
As ignorant as dirt! Thou hast done a deed –
I care not for thy sword; I'll make thee known,
Though I lost twenty lives. – Help! Help, ho! Help!
The Moor hath kill'd my mistress! Murder! murder!

Enter IAGO, MONTANO, LODOVICO, BIANCA and CASSIO.

EMILIA

O, are you come, Iago? You have done well,
That men must lay their murders on your neck.
Disprove this villain, if thou be'st a man:
He says thou told'st him that his wife was false:
I know thou didst not, thou'rt not such a villain:
Speak, for my heart is full.

IAGO

I told him what I thought, and told no more
Than what he found himself was apt and true.

EMILIA

But did you ever tell him she was false?

IAGO

I did.

EMILIA

You told a lie, an odious, damned lie;
Upon my soul, a lie, a wicked lie.
She false with Cassio! – Did you say with Cassio?

IAGO

With Cassio, mistress. Go to, charm your tongue.

EMILIA

I will not charm my tongue; I am bound to speak:
My mistress here lies murder'd
And your reports have set the murder on.

OTHELLO

Nay, stare not, masters: it is true, indeed.

MONTANO

'Tis a strange truth.

EMILIA

Villany, villany, villany!
I think upon't, I think: I smell't: O villany!
I thought so then: I'll kill myself for grief.

IAGO

What, are you mad? I charge you, get you home.

EMILIA
I will ne'er home. Good gentlemen, let me have leave to speak:
Now, lay thee down and roar;
For thou hast kill'd the sweetest innocent
That e'er did lift up eye.

OTHELLO
'Tis pitiful; but yet Iago knows
That she with Cassio hath the act of shame
A thousand times committed; Cassio confess'd it:
And she did gratify his amorous works
With that recognizance and pledge of love
Which I first gave her; I saw it in his hand:
It was a handkerchief.

EMILIA
(*Intercutting.*) O God!

IAGO
Hold your peace.

EMILIA
'Twill out, 'twill out: I peace!
No, I will speak as liberal as the north.

IAGO
Be wise…

EMILIA
Let heaven and men and devils, let them all,
All, all, cry shame against me, yet I'll speak.

IAGO
Be wise, and get you home.

EMILIA
I will not.
O thou dull Moor! That handkerchief thou speak'st of
I found by fortune and did give my husband;

IAGO smashes a bottle and stabs EMILIA.

IAGO
Villanous whore!

IAGO tries to exit but is held by MONTANO and LODOVICO.

EMILIA

Moor, she was chaste, she loved thee.
She loved thee.

OTHELLO

O Precious Villain!

OTHELLO wounds IAGO.

IAGO

I bleed, sir; but not kill'd.

OTHELLO

I am not sorry neither: I'd have thee live;
For, in my sense, 'tis happiness to die.

LODOVICO

O thou Othello, thou wert once so good,
Fall'n in the practice of a damned slave,
What shall be said to thee?

OTHELLO

Why, any thing:
An honourable murderer, if you will;
For nought I did in hate, but all in honour.

LODOVICO

This wretch hath part confess'd his villany:
Did you and he consent in Cassio's death?

OTHELLO

Ay.

CASSIO

Dear general, I never gave you cause.

OTHELLO

I do believe it, and I ask your pardon.
Will you, I pray, demand that demi-devil
Why he hath thus ensnared my soul and body?

IAGO

Demand me nothing: what you know, you know:
From this time forth I never will speak word.

OTHELLO

How came you, Cassio, by that handkerchief
That was my wife's?

CASSIO

I found it on my person.

OTHELLO

O fool! Fool! Fool!
When you shall these unlucky deeds relate,
Speak of me as I am; nothing extenuate,
Nor set down aught in malice: then must you speak
Of one that loved not wisely but too well;
Of one not easily jealous, but being wrought
Perplex'd in the extreme.

LODOVICO

You must forsake this room.

LODOVICO and MONTANO push OTHELLO into the women's toilets.

His power and his command is taken off,
And Cassio rules The Cypress.
For this slave,
If there be any cunning cruelty
That can torment him much and hold him long,
It shall be his.

MONTANO attacks IAGO. There is a smash of glass off. MONTANO and LODOVICO stop the attack. They turn to see OTHELLO. He has returned into the room. He has a shard of glass in this hand and he is covered in blood.

Lights up on the women's toilet. The mirror has been smashed and the sink and walls are covered in blood. OTHELLO has cut his wrists.

OTHELLO

Be not afraid, though you do see me weapon'd;
Here is my journey's end,
And very sea-mark of my utmost sail.
I kiss'd thee ere I kill'd thee: no way but this;
Killing myself, to die upon a kiss.

Falls on the pool table, and dies.

LODOVICO

O Spartan dog,
More fell than anguish, hunger, or the sea!
Look on the tragic loading of this bed;
This is thy work.

The walls part as MONTANO and LODOVICO drag IAGO outside and give him a kicking.

Inside, BIANCA is held by CASSIO as they attempt to comfort one another.

The End.